Air Commodore M. Zafar Masud – A Pioneer of the Pakistan Air Force

*Story of the Man who Sacrificed
His Career in an Effort to Save Pakistan*

Nasim Yousaf

Published by:
AMZ Publications
New York, USA

Table of Contents

Dedication

This work is dedicated to Air Commodore Mohammad Zafar Masud. He was a recipient of the *Hilal-e-Jurat* and *Sitara-e-Basalat*.[1] A page on Facebook has also been dedicated to him.[2]

I would also like to dedicate this work to my daughter, Mehreen.

Acknowledgement

I would like to extend a special thanks to those who have written informative pieces on Air Commodore M. Zafar Masud, including Air Chief Marshal (Retd.) Jamal A. Khan and Usman Sadiq (Pilot), whose work I have quoted in this publication.

I also extend my cordial thanks to all other learned persons, whose material I have used in this work.

Tributes

"Masud led us through the hazards of combat flying with the same energy and disregard for danger as he showed in his spirited embrace of Karachi's social milieu. Ever visible was the infectious idealism - the reason for his nickname, an allusion to the fictional Walter Mitty - that drove him to set for himself and his subordinates difficult-to-achieve standards."[3]

— Air Chief Marshal (Retd.) Jamal A. Khan

***

Air Commodore Zafar Masud "was and probably, has been, the most brilliant planner and professional commander ever produced by PAF, who very ably led the air battle from Sargodha in 1965 War. I had the highest regards and respect for him."[4]

— Air Marshal (Retd.) Inam-ul-Haq Khan

***

"Air Commodores (late) Masroor Hussain, M.Z. Masood [Zafar Masud], and (late) F.S. Hussain became legends during their life time."[5]

— Air Marshal (Retd.) Ayaz Ahmed Khan

***

"Mitty Masud or Air Commodore…was larger than life and I really don't know where to start. …To us young aspiring civilian pilots he was the ultimate instructor [at the Rawalpindi Flying Club]. For those of us who had more a passion for flying than just our CPL it was a matter of honor, pride & a bit of glamour to be able to fly with him. One couldn't just fly with him…one had to be taken in by him. I used the good offices of my mother's chacha and a very good friend of his Air Commodore (Retd) Mir Riffat Mehmood to put in a word for me."[6]

— Usman Sadiq (a pilot)

***

"During the 1965 war, as commanding officer of Sargodha Base, Group Captain [Air Commodore] Masud showed great qualities of leadership, devotion to duty and organising ability in the conduct of air operations against the enemy.

…he won awards for leading a formation of 16 Sabre jet aircraft in a vertical loop, a world record."[7]

— The *Daily Times* (October 08, 2003), Lahore, Pakistan reporting on Air Commodore Masud's death

***

"In the 1965 War, Sargodha proved to be the most important PAF base and played a decisive role in the defence of Pakistan with its spectacular performance under Group Captain Zafar Masud. Soon after that war, Chinese F-6s joined the PAF inventory and again Sargodha Base was the first to receive these aircraft. This event was closely followed by yet another induction, the French Mirage-III, which replaced 5 Squadron's Sabres…"[8] — PAF Falcons

About the Author

Nasim Yousaf, a well-known scholar and historian, has been in research in the USA since 1996. He has thus far published 14 books and compiled many rare and historical works including the *Al-Islah* weekly newspaper of his grandfather, Allama Mashriqi, which was founded in 1934. His works have been published in the prestigious journals *Education About Asia* (a teaching journal published in USA), *Harvard Asia Quarterly* and *Pakistaniaat* (USA) as well as in the *World History Encyclopedia* (USA). He has presented papers at academic and scholarly conferences in the U.S. He has also published numerous articles which have appeared in newspapers in many countries, including Australia, Bangladesh, Canada, Hong Kong (China), Pakistan, India, Japan, Norway, United Kingdom, and the USA. His books and other works are important contributions to the historiography of South Asia. Some of his published works include:

- *Allama Mashriqi Narrowly Escapes the Gallows: Court Proceedings of an Unpardonable Crime Against the Man Who Led the Freedom of the Indian Subcontinent*

- *Mahatma Gandhi & My Grandfather, Allama Mashriqi: A Groundbreaking Narrative of India's Partition*

- *Hidden Facts Behind British India's Freedom: A Scholarly Look into Allama Mashraqi and Quaid-e-Azam's Political Conflict*

- *Dr. Akhtar Hameed Khan - Pioneer of Microcredit & Guru of Rural Development*

***

The author had met Air Commodore Mohammad Zafar Masud and his wife Elizabeth Masud.

According to the author, Nasim Yousaf:

> "I used to learn about respected Air Commodore Masud from his mother, Zakia Sultana (who was my mother's first cousin), during her periodic visits to our house. She used to speak about the fascinating and inspiring stories of her son's achievements in the PAF and this built in me a great desire to meet him.
>
> After retirement, Air Commodore Masud (who happened to be my second cousin) came to Abbottabad Club and stayed there for some time. I went to see him, and over afternoon tea and dinner spent some memorable hours speaking with him and his wife. I remember them to be persons of good nature and taste. I remember Air Cdr. Masud to be a highly cultured, handsome and a very impressive personality. He had a strong command of English and was pretty good in German. His wife, who was German, could speak English and Urdu as well. She was a key and very active member of the PAF Women's Association. Air Cdr. Masud and his wife took keen interest in improving the conditions of

poor employees and their children. Their contributions within the PAF are well-known. I have cherished memories of both.

Air Cdr. Masud's love for the PAF was visible from the fact that he recommended I join the Pakistan Air Force. Though I was more interested in joining the Army, Air Cdr. Masud's recommendation swayed me and I soon joined the Air Force myself. Though this was a great and cherished profession, it did not fit my dreams and passion in life, and therefore I resigned a bit before I was about to be promoted from Pilot Officer to Flying Officer."

***

For updates on the author's published and forthcoming works, visit:

- https://www.facebook.com/nasimyousaf.26
- https://www.scribd.com/NasimYousaf

Chapter 1: The Pakistan Air Force is Born

Before we begin the narrative about Air Commodore Mohammad Zafar Masud,[9] it is important to understand how the Pakistan Air Force came into being.

Early Origins of the Pakistan Air Force (PAF)

Back in 1914,[10] the foundation of the Royal Air Force in India was laid by forming the Royal Flying Corps, a small organization. The Indian Air Force (IAF) was formed later on April 01, 1933.[11] In this same year, the first batch of Indian cadets was sent for training to Royal Air Force College, Cranwell, in England.[12] By 1942, the IAF had four squadrons[13] and with time, it grew much bigger. The IAF provided tremendous services to the British in World War II, and in 1945 the pre-fix "Royal" was added to "Indian Air Force" – it then became known as the Royal Indian Air Force (RIAF).

The Royal Indian Air Force was strategically important for the British rulers, not only for maintenance of their rule over the Indian sub-continent but for use of the said organization wherever and whenever needed. The Royal Indian Air Force had for instance greatly contributed during World War II to the defeat of the Japanese invasion.[14] And it is on record that RIAF men fought the rulers' wars in different parts of the world. In addition, the RIAF supplied all kinds of raw-material to the British defense industries.[15]

1947: The Partition of India and Division of Assets

In August 1947, British India was divided. Thus, Pakistan and India emerged on August 14 and August 15, 1947, respectively.

The Royal Pakistan Air Force (RPAF) was born on the midnight[16] of August 14, 1947. Air Vice Marshal A.L.A. Perry Keene was appointed as the first Commander of the newly born RPAF. Its Headquarters were kept at Peshawar in North West Frontier (NWFP), now *Khyber Pakhtunkhwa*.

With the emergence of two sovereign States, the issue of dividing the assets of the Royal Indian Air Force arose and a tussle began between the two new countries.[17] Owing to the locations of the equipment, manpower as well as other military paraphernalia, this was not a simple matter. This is evident from *The Pakistan Times* daily report: "A senior Indian Air Force Officer said, the Air Force would offer the greatest difficulty from the view point of division..."[18]

Deliberations continued on the division of assets in the Partition Council; however, these were matters that could not be settled instantly. A month later, *The Pakistan Times* reported:

> "Final decisions have now been reached by the Partition Council for the reconstitution of the Armed Forces between the future Governments of India and Pakistan, says a communique...

Recommendations regarding the reconstitution
of the Royal Indian Air Force and some units
of the Indian Army have not yet been made to
the Partition Council."[19]

Once decisions on the distribution of assets were finally
made, the RPAF was highly dissatisfied. According to
RPAF, this division was not equal and injustice had been
done to Pakistan. The following extract is taken from the
PAF website which is self-explanatory:

"...India with an inherent resentment towards
the creation of Pakistan tried to subvert our
capabilities by crippling Pakistan militarily. It
denied the then Royal Pakistan Air Force
(RPAF) even the officially agreed small
portions of weapons, equipment and aircraft
allocated by departing British as its legitimate
share. Much of what was eventually received
from India was inoperable. Crates of
equipment contained nothing but scrap and
waste. The RPAF got 16 fighter aircraft as its
foundation. It started off with one squadron of
eight Tempest aircraft and a small remnant of
No 1 Squadron Royal Indian Air Force (RIAF)
which was subsequently utilized to raise No 5
Squadron."[20]

The Royal Pakistan Air Force inherited 5, 6, and 9
squadrons, number 301 maintenance unit and the RPAF
stations namely Chaklala (Rawalpindi, Punjab), Drig
Road (Karachi, Sind), Kohat (NWFP Province now
Khyber Pakhtunkhwa), Korangi Creek (Karachi, Sind),
Lahore (Punjab), Malir (Sind), Peshawar (Khyber
Pakhtunkhwa), and Risalpur (Khyber Pakhtunkhwa).[21]

With regard to distribution of personnel, approximately 220 officers and 2112 airmen opted for transfer to RPAF. Among these were 197 Muslims, 11 Anglo-Pakistanis, 10 Christians, and 2 Hindus.[22] See endnote for additional reported figures.[23]

Pioneer Officers of the RPAF

A great challenge lay ahead for the Royal Pakistan Air Force, particularly in comparison to the Royal Indian Air Force, as it had to be built up from scratch. There was a general lack of funds, infrastructure and professional expertise needed to raise a military organization. The personnel comprised of pilots, navigators, engineers, doctors, lawyer, administrators, accountants, and technicians. However, despite their qualifications on an individual level, they had no experience running an independent entity — that too an entire country's air force — and were very few in number relative to the country's size.

A daunting task lay ahead for RPAF officers and personnel. Air Cdr. Mohammad Zafar Masud (then Pilot Officer), the junior most pilot was not yet twenty years old.[24] He and others began working day and night to raise the RPAF to the highest professional levels. A Chapter entitled "Assembly of the Pioneers" in the book *The Story of the Pakistan Air Force — A Saga of Courage and Honour* sheds light on the state of the newly born RPAF.[25]

According to the Pakistan Air Force's official web site:

"...Most of these unsung heroes, toiled relentlessly on an arduous task to set the foundation of an air force that in the years to come, would be reckoned as one of the best in the world. Semi trained, ill equipped and faced with an enemy much larger in size, they worked with great zeal and fervor, often faced with a daunting task of keeping their flying machines aloft.

These men came from different air stations of RIAF, some battle hardened others novice in their trade, converged on to their pre-designated reporting points in their homeland - Pakistan..."[26]

The site also names some of these individuals including the following:

- *Pilots:* Mohammad Khan Janjua, Haider Raza, Maqbool Rabb, Abdul Rehman (all had held senior command or staff appointments in the RIAF). Asghar Khan (on July 23, 1957, Air Vice Marshal (later Air Marshal), Asghar Khan become the first Commander in Chief (C-in-C) of Pakistan Air Force at the age of about 37 years). Nur Khan, Mohammad Akhtar, 'Steve' Joseph, Khyber Khan, Abdul Qadir, Eric Hall, Rahim Khan, Zafar Chaudhry, Masroor Hosain, F S Hussain, Saeedullah Khan, Rab Nawaz, Mick' O'Brian, **'Mitty' Masud (Air Commodore M. Zafar Masud)**
- *Navigators:* Kamal Ahmed, 'T S' Jan, Air gunner Alfred Jagjivan

- *Engineers:* 'Jerry' Khan, Mohammad Mahboob, 'Chacha' Siddique, Khalilur Razzak, 'Musti' Khan
- *Administrative Officers:* Mofazil Alahdad, Mahbub Piracha
- *Meteorologists:* Hidayatullah, Abdul Qadir
- *Doctor:* Riffat Mahmood
- *Educationist:* Asghar Hussain
- *Legal Specialist:* Mohammad Aslam[27]

A complete list of pioneering officers is provided on the PAF website.[28]

Building the Royal Pakistan Air Force

From 1947-1954,[29] most of the RPAF equipment was of British origin. However in 1955,[30] the RPAF looked toward the USA for assistance (more on aid[31]). The United States Air Force (USAF) not only trained RPAF personnel but also provided modern equipment and aircrafts. According to the book entitled, *The Story of the Pakistan Air Force — A Saga of Courage and Honour*:

> "It [PAF] would remain deeply indebted to the USAF for introducing it to the latest concepts in combat training, in the organisation of maintenance, in operational planning, in the attainment of sound safety standards; all these factors played a major part in enabling the PAF to give its giant adversary a bloody nose in that war."[32]

On March 23, 1956 (Pakistan Republic Day), the prefix "Royal" was removed and the air force came to be known as the Pakistan Air Force (PAF). The change of name was celebrated with a grand display at Drig Road at Karachi.

By 1958, the PAF had established itself and sought recognition. A United Kingdom magazine called *The Aeroplane* wrote an article on PAF entitled, "The Pakistan Air Force."

> The said piece stated: "The Pakistan Air Force is not large by European standards, but it must be reckoned as one of the most highly trained and efficient units in Southern Asia..."[33]

By 1958, the PAF was also training men in various areas, including foreign pilots as well as members of the national airline (Pakistan International Airlines).

> "Among the students on Sabre courses...were three pilots from the Royal Jordanian Air Force, who are to fly with the P.A.F. for a few months. The training is also undertaken of a few apprentices and mechanics for Pakistan International Airlines..."[34]

The dedicated pioneering team, which had established the Pakistan Air Force given significant challenges, deserves tremendous applause. The credit also goes to the USAF which contributed a great deal to the PAF. Without the USAF's training and superior quality equipment, the PAF would not have been where it is today.

Chapter 2: Air Commodore Mohammad Zafar Masud – Early-Mid Career

"The late Air Commodore M. Zafar Masud helped to mould the Pakistan Air Force into an effective fighting machine. Pakistan will remember him as one who made a great contribution towards the development of the Pakistan Air Force and thus to the defence of Pakistan in the 1965 war. Air Commodore M Zafar Masud always set an example in the performance of his duties."[35]

— Air Marshal (Retd.) Asghar Khan

"An exceptional fighter pilot, Masud was at his best when given really challenging assignments, but even when asked to take on some mundane tasks he tackled those with great energy and inventiveness. Quite remarkably, within days of taking over a new unit, the men under him would begin to identify with his goals, and the experience always left them better trained and stronger advocates of professional values."[36]

— Air Chief Marshal (Retd.) Jamal A. Khan

Air Commodore Mohammad Zafar Masud was affectionately known as "Mitty Masud" in the Pakistan Air Force. He obtained commission in the GD (P) branch of the Royal Indian Air Force in British India on February 25, 1946 and his service number (allotted to each officer) was 3314.[37] In 1947, at the time of partition of British

India, officers were asked to choose between Pakistan and India, and Air Cdr. Masud opted for Pakistani citizenship. In his early career, he commanded No. 5 and No. 11 squadrons (see appendices for more information on these squadrons) of the PAF.

From the start of his time in the PAF, Air Cdr. Masud was dedicated to the building of the force. He was regarded as a legendary and courageous pilot. Air Chief Marshal Jamal A. Khan in his article ("Mitty Masud folds his wings") called him an "exceptional fighter pilot" and a "war hero."[38] Air Chief Marshal Anwar Shamim in his book ranked him "top-rated fighter pilot."[39] Air Cdr. Masud was also a recipient of the prestigious awards, *Hilal-e-Jurat* and *Sitara-e-Basalat.*

The following narrative tells the story of Air Commodore Masud's early to mid- career and highlights some of the major milestones of his professional life.

Early in His Career – Air Commodore Masud Sets a World Record

Air Cdr. Masud stood out from early in his career and managed to create history on February 02, 1958. He was then Wing Commander, and at about 10' clock in the morning on this date, he led a formation of Sabre jets — 16 Sabres of the Pakistan Air Force went into a loop and created a precise pattern in the shape of a diamond in the sky.

The team comprised of Zafar Masud, Middlecoat, Sadruddin, W. Azim, Aftab Ahmed, S.M. Ahmed, G.

Haider, Lodhi, Jamal Khan, M. Arshad, Munir, H. Anwar, S.U. Khan, N. Latif, A.U. Ahmed, and S.S. Haider.[40]

Syed Shabbir Hussain and M. Tariq Qureshi wrote in their book:

> "Sixteen Sabres took off in groups of four, the formation team being led by Wg. Cdr. (later Air Commodore), M. Z. Masud...The sixteen 'Falcons' which had positioned themselves then went into the breathtaking maneuver of a formation loop. All through, the aircraft maintained immaculate station and precise diamond pattern. A new record was created; for the first time in the history of aviation such a large number of aircraft had performed a loop in close formation."[41]

This ceremony was attended by more than 30,000[42] spectators and many dignitaries, such as the President of Pakistan Iskander Mirza, King of Afghanistan Mohammad Zahir Shah[43](Chief Guest), and Commander Chiefs of the Iranian, Iraqi and Turkish Air Forces (Maj-Gen. H. Gilenshah, Imperial Iranian Air Force; Brig. K. Abbadi, Royal Iraqi Air Force; Lt.Gen. Hamidullah Suphi Gokar, Turkish Air Force) as well as representatives of the Royal Jordanian Air Force.[44] The venue resounded with claps and applauds for Air Cdr. Masud and his team.

Not only were the dignitaries highly impressed with the young organization and professionalism of the pilots, but the news spread around the world. *The Aeroplane*, a famous U.K. magazine, wrote a complete article on the event entitled, "Pakistan Shows its Sabres." An extract is as follows:

"...the *pie'ce de re'sistance* of the P.A.F. flying display, which was a formation loop by no fewer than 16 Sabres, more jet aircraft, it is believed, than have previously flown together in aerobatic manoeuvres...

...By European standards it is most unusual to be able to see this manoeuvre by transonic aircraft...

...The 16 Sabres of the 'Falcon' aerobatic team, led by Wg. Cdr. M. Z. Masud, then came in at about 5,000 ft. to start their loop in diamond formation, which was maintained impeccably throughout the manoeuvre. It was a highly accomplished feat of flying, completed with an efficiency equal to any air force in the World."[45]

This world record brought tremendous honor and recognition to the PAF as well as Pakistan. Air Chief Marshal Jamal A. Khan wrote:

"In 1958 Air Marshal Asghar Khan chose Wing Commander Masud to organize, train and lead an aerobatics team of 16 Sabre jets that set a world record, validating the PAF's place among the well- regarded air arms of the world." [46]

Founder of Combat Commanders' School

The newly appointed Commander-in-Chief of the Pakistan Air Force, Air Vice-Marshal M. Asghar Khan (later Air Marshal), realized Air Cdr. Masud's (then Wing

Commander) exceptional abilities, and after this event, he asked Masud to form a training institute to advance Pakistani pilots' flying and leadership skills to world class.

Air Cdr. Masud worked hard and in May 1958, he founded the Fighter Leaders' School[47] (which is now known as the Combat Commanders' School, CCS). At school, he delivered lectures and taught aircraft maneuvers, combat techniques and strategies to pilots. With his dedication, he converted CCS to one of the best fighter pilot schools in the world. Many pilots under his guidance and leadership emerged as the best and most skilled fighter pilots of PAF. The CCS continues to provide very rigorous training to experienced fighter pilots and air defense controllers at PAF Base Mushaf (formerly PAF Base Sargodha).

> "This fighter tactics and weapons school is the Pakistani equivalent of the American 'Topgun' school at US Naval Air Station Miramar in California. CCS is a most coveted Fighter School in PAF."[48]

> The CCS "first came to prominence during the Indo-Pakistan Wars of 1965 and 1971..." and the said institution "...earned it the reputation of the [US] 'Top Gun' base of the Pakistan Air Force."[49]

In October 1958, Air Cdr. Masud (then Wing Commander) was appointed as the Commander of Fighter Ground Attack (F.G.A) No 32. Meanwhile, he was selected and sent to England to Royal Air Force College

Cranwell to take a Staff College course; he returned with a "best foreign student award."[50]

Promoted to Base Commander PAF Base Sargodha (now Mushaf)

On December 18, 1963, Air Cdr. Masud was promoted to Group Captain and given the command of PAF Base Sargodha, one of the most important and central bases of PAF.[51] The posting to PAF Base Sargodha was considered to be a prize posting. He held command of the said base for longer than anyone else at the time. As usual, Air Cdr. Masud dedicated his time and effort and greatly improved the base and the professionalism of the pilots and staff. He significantly influenced the base's defensive and offensive capabilities, empowering it to handle and undertake attack more effectively. According to the book *History of the Pakistan Air Force (1947-1982)*:

> "He geared up PAF Sargodha to optimum performance level and when war came in September, 1965, Sargodha was ready to face the challenge."[52]

A few months prior to the September 1965 war with India, on May 20, 1965, the President of Pakistan Mohammad Ayub Khan came to Sargodha Base and assessed the improvements achieved under Air Cdr. Masud's (then Group Captain) command. The President left highly impressed.

> To witness his achievements, "There were three visits by the newly appointed C-in-C

PAF, Air Vice-Marshal M. Nur Khan in August, 1965. A.O.C. Air Defence Air Commodore Masroor Hosain also visited Sargodha during the same month."[53]

Sargodha Base Creates World Record

Sargodha was the leading and most vital operational station of the Pakistan Air Force. On 5th September, 1965, Air Marshal Asghar Khan (then recently retired) arrived from Chaklala to evaluate the war situation. Air Commodore Masud was working without proper sleep and food. Air Marshal Asghar Khan was impressed by Air Cdr. Masud's command and control and his readiness to face any challenge.

In September, a full-fledged war between Pakistan and India began. India was aware of the Sargodha Base's importance and Air Commodore Masud's commanding abilities. Thus, his base was attacked heavily, but Air Cdr. Masud was prepared. During the war, he led an extremely busy life. He was occupied with planning strategies to ensure that the enemy did not succeed in its designs and that he ensured his base's success. According to a book edited by Rais Ahmad Jafri:

> "Sitting in his overalls with no rank badges on his shoulders, the 38 year old Commander, was busy with the phone giving instructions in base, grave and confident voice when I crawled into his tent...
>
> I pulled myself up and saluted the famous Commander. ...the cool organizational ability

of this man who at the helm of affairs led his
men with rare courage and determination.

…He has been in that chair for two days and
two nights moving only between the chair and
the trench behind it. His normally shining eyes
had been dulled by prolonged sleeplessness.
His fair complexion had turned sallow.

There were scores of telephones and intercoms
spread all around him. He attended half a
dozen of them before he could attend to me
with a smile and a stern 'hello.'…He was too
busy a man."[54]

During the 1965 war, many pilots of the Sargodha Base,
under Air Cdr. Masud's command, performed extremely
well. As an example, on September 7, 1965, Sargodha
Base inflicted "crippling defeat upon IAF [Indian Air
Force] in air combats."[55] Famous pilot, Air Commodore
(then squadron leader) M.M. Alam (Mohammad
Mahmood Alam) of 11 Squadron based at Sargodha, shot
down five Indian fighter aircrafts in less than a minute[56]
— the first four within 30 seconds — establishing a world
record. For his outstanding performance, Air Cdr. Alam
was awarded *Sitara-e-Jurat.*[57] Wing Commander
Muhammad Anwar Shamim (then officer commanding of
Number 33 Wing, later Air Chief Marshal and Chief of
the Air Staff of the PAF) was honored with *Sitara-e-
Jurat.* Similarly, Flight Lieutenant Syed Saad Akhtar
Hatmi and Flight Lieutenant Yusuf Ali Khan were also
awarded *Sitara-e-Jurat.* Sqn Ldr. Sarfaraz Ahmad
Rafiqui, Commander of Squadron No. 5 Sargodha, led a
formation of three F-86 aircrafts on September 6, 1965 in
a strike against IAF's strongly defended Halwara
airfield; he was awarded *Sitara-e-Jurat* and later *Hilal-e-*

Jurat. Flt. Lt (later Air Commodore) Imtiaz Ahmed Bhatti was given *Sitara-e-Jurat*, and Flt. Lt. (later Group Captain) Cecil Chaudhry was awarded *Sitara-e-Jurat*. Flt. Lt. Amjad Hussain Khan was also awarded *Sitara-e-Jurat.*

Syed Shabbir Hussain and M. Tariq Qureshi wrote in their book:

> "In 1965, the air war was primarily fought and won at Sargodha... All squadron pilots put up a commendable performance; amongst the outstanding were Sqn. Ldr. M.M. Alam, Flt. Lt. Saad Hatmi [Syed Saad Akhtar Hatmi], Flt. Lt. Yusuf Ali Khan and Flt Lt. Jillani [Syed Nazir Ahmed Jilani]...The officers who were awarded combat decorations included Sq. Ldr. M.M. Alam (Sitara-e-Jurat with Bar), Flt. Lt. S.A. Hatmi [Syed Saad Akhtar Hatmi] (Sitara-e-Jurat), and Flt. Lt. Yusuf A. Khan (Sitara-e-Jurat)."[58]

The success of the pilots was not possible without Air Cdr. Masud's strategic planning, training and guidance, and motivation to keep up morale. His base emerged as the most successful among the PAF during the war with India and news of its excellent performance spread all over. Air Commodore Masud was recognized as an outstanding commander and hero; Air Marshal Ayaz Ahmed Khan wrote in his article:

> "The outstanding leadership of Air Commodore M.Z. Masud, Base Commander of PAF Sargodha at the time, enhanced the high morale and motivation of the fighter pilots and the technicians during the war."[59]

According to a book edited by Rais Ahmad Jafri:

> "I congratulated him on the performance of his situation which he accepted with a modest smile. When requested for an interview he like a true commander said that 'the real heroes are the officers and men of the station who have worked day and night during these hours of trial.'"[60]

According to the book entitled *History of the Pakistan Air Force: 1947-1982*:

> "As Commanding Officer of the most important operational station of the Pakistan Air Force, Group Captain Mohammad Zafar Masud showed great qualities of leadership, devotion to duty and organizing ability, in the conduct of air operations against the enemy. On the day and night of the 7th September, 1965 in particular, when the enemy made five successive attacks on the airfield and its installation with Canberra bombers, Hunters and Mystere fighter bombers, the cool courage and determination with which the whole Station faced the attacks and the heavy damage inflicted by its fighters on the enemy aircraft clearly indicated the high morale and professional efficiency achieved by the station personnel under the command of Group Captain Masud."[61]

The reason Air Cdr. Masud was highly praised was because despite the shortcomings and limitations of the Sargodha Base, as compared to the much bigger Indian Air Force, Air Cdr. Masud was able to elevate the base's capabilities and attacked the enemy with such marvelous planning and skills that startled everyone, including the Indian Air Force. An Indian Fighter Pilot graciously acknowledged Air Cdr. Masud's performance and planning:

> India Air Force Officer, Wing Commander (Retd.) RA Rufus KC wrote: "…When Pakistan made that Crescent attack led by my course mate Mohammed Zafar Masud and we lost 18 aircraft on the ground…"[62]

President Mohammad Ayub Khan along with General Muhammad Musa of the Pakistan Army visited Sargodha Base and praised Air Commodore Masud for his outstanding planning and performance. On this occasion, Air Cdr. Masud introduced pilots and other staff members under his command, including the famous and legendary pilot Air Cdr. M. M. Alam.

> "It was here that Group Captain Masud, Commander of the base, presented Squadron Leader Muhammad Mahmud Alam [M.M. Alam], who was congratulated by the President. The PAF hero [M.M. Alam] also met General Muhammad Musa."[63]

Given the performance of the PAF Base Sargodha, September 7 was declared "Pakistan Air Force Day." In addition, due to Air Cdr. Masud's "success of the Pakistan Air Force operations against the enemy since the commencement of the War"[64], he was awarded the *second highest military award of Pakistan Hilal-e-Jurat*, which is one step behind the top *Nishan-i-Haider* (this is not given to a live person). He was one of the three[65] recipients of this award in the PAF.

According to a book edited by Rais Ahmad Jafri:

> "The most signal contribution to this was made by the Commander of the PAF base which faced the heaviest brunt of the enemy aggression.

> ...suave and handsome group-captain Muhammad Zafar Masud was awarded the Hilal-i-Jur'at for 'exceptional qualities of leadership, devotion to duty and organising ability in the conduct of air operations against the enemy.'"[66]

The *Pakistan Review* also published a list of names of personnel of the Pakistan Armed Forces entitled, "Gallery of National Heroes" and included Air Commodore Masud's name.[67]

Promoted to Air Commodore & Appointed Air Officer Commanding (AOC) East Pakistan

M. Zafar Masud was rising in his career and was considered the *future head of the Pakistan Air Force*. After the war, he was promoted to the rank of Air Commodore. In February 1968,[68] he was given another important assignment and posted to Air Head Quarters of PAF as the Assistant Chief of Air Staff (Operations).

The same year, he was included as part of the Pakistan Armed Forces Goodwill Delegation to China. The deputation comprised of General Agha Mohammad Yahya Khan (then Commander-in-Chief of the Pakistan Army, later President of Pakistan), Major General Mohammad Akbar Khan, Brigadier Mohammad Akram, Commodore M. Shariff, and Air Commodore M. Zafar Masud. Upon arrival at Beijing / Peking on November 8, 1968, the officers were given a "rousing welcome." On November 10, 1968, Chairman Mao Tse-tung (Mao Zedong) met all members of the delegation. Present on the occasion were Chou En-lai, Kang Sheng, Huang Yung-sheng (Chief of the General Staff of the Chinese People's Liberation Army), Wu Fa-hsien, Sultan M. Khan (Pakistan Ambassador to China), and other Pakistani diplomatic officials of the Pakistani Embassy in China.[69]

In the early 1970s, Air Cdr. Masud was again awarded *Sitara-e-Basalat.*

In April 1970, Air Cdr. Masud was posted to East Pakistan (now Bangladesh) as the Base Commander Dhaka (Dacca); later, he was also appointed as the Air Officer Commanding East Pakistan.[70] In 1971, he was appointed as the Unified Commander of Eastern Military High Command, controlling the Air Force, Navy, and Army — he was the first Pakistan Air Force officer to assume the said command.

Air Commodore Masud's posting to East Pakistan was a tough assignment. The air force capability in East Pakistan was very small compared to that in West Pakistan and he was selected for this assignment given his record of success. His appointment to East Pakistan was not only a hard assignment, but would prove to be a turning point in his career.

Chapter 3: 1970 Elections & The Political Turmoil in East Pakistan

Introduction

The early 1970s was a major era in Pakistan's history – with great turmoil in East Pakistan and circumstances which eventually led to the breakup of East Pakistan from West. Air Commodore Masud's posting to East Pakistan during this time challenged him not only physically and mentally, but morally. Air Cdr. Masud — a pioneer of the Pakistan Air Force — had a promising career ahead, but faced a dilemma which eventually led him to sacrifice his career.

The Political Situation in East Pakistan Leading up to the 70s – Air Commodore Masud Posted to East Wing

Since partition in 1947, the political situation in East Pakistan had been unstable. Pakistan had been divided into two parts – East and West – with the vast country of India in the middle. In addition to the expected challenges associated with a geographically split country, resentment in East Pakistan began to grow as West Pakistan seemed to dominate in all spheres. For instance, the Bengali peoples' demand of making the Bengali language, widely spoken in the East wing, a national/official language was not accepted by Quaid-e-Azam Mohammad Ali Jinnah, founder of Pakistan.

Moreover, major investment and industrialization were undertaken in the West wing. The distribution of income towards East Pakistan was not only discriminatory, but the income earned through East Pakistan's resources was also directed towards the West wing. Key jobs in the Government sector were mainly reserved for the West Pakistanis. Such behavior right from country's emergence in 1947 and in the later years brought tremendous resentment towards West Pakistan. The Government of Pakistan based in the West did nothing substantial to redress the situation and continued with such policies. Thus, over a period of time, the situation in East Pakistan went from bad to worse.

After the 1965 war between Pakistan and India, Zulfiqar Ali Bhutto (who founded Pakistan's People's Party in 1967) started campaigning against President Ayub Khan, shortly after resigning from Ayub Khan's cabinet. Sheikh Mujibur Rahman (President of the Awami League, a political party) also started an insurgency. It is important to note that before 1949, Mujibur Rahman had been part of the All-India Muslim League, which supported the partition of India (and creation of Pakistan as a separate state) in 1947 (against the wishes of majority of Muslims and non-Muslims). However, after the creation of Pakistan, due to the discriminatory policies of West Pakistan as described earlier, he developed major grievances against West Pakistan. Thus, he also decided to exploit the situation to gain political benefit and began encouraging an insurgency. As an aside, Mujibur Rahman was also in contact with India for potential intervention and support.

Bhutto, Mujibur Rahman and others, began to campaign against President Ayub Khan and demanded country-wide elections. Ayub Khan arrested both of them (they were later released). The ongoing protests and political turmoil in the country ultimately led Ayub Khan to resign. In 1969, Ayub Khan voluntarily handed over power to the Commander-in-Chief of the Pakistan Army, General Agha Mohammad Yahya Khan, who imposed Martial Law in the country, became President of Pakistan and promised to hold free and fair elections.

During this time, the Pakistan Air Force in East Pakistan was not organized or well-equipped. It was anticipated that there may be turmoil and a possibility of aggression or intervention from India. As a precautionary step, Air Cdr. Masud, with his background as one of the top officers, was sent to East Pakistan in April 1970 to transform the Air Force into a well-organized body capable of meeting any aggression mainly from outside the country.

The 1970s – Start of Major Conflict

On December 07, 1970, for the first time in the history of Pakistan, free and fair general elections were held under the auspices of President of Pakistan, Agha Mohammad Yahya Khan. Sheikh Mujibur Rahman's political party (Awami League) earned a clear victory (160 out of 162 seats in East Pakistan) in the elections and emerged as the leading party. Upon this sweeping victory, Sheikh Mujibur Rahman was confident to become the Prime Minister of Pakistan (provided he would be voted to the position in the National Assembly). His confidence can be gauged from the fact that he sent Dr. Kamal (a very close associate of Sheikh Mujibur Rahman) to Comilla to meet Dr. Akhtar Hameed Khan (who was very well-respected throughout East Pakistan and was known for bringing about the Green Revolution in Bangladesh) to discuss future developing projects in East Pakistan. Dr. Kamal stayed at Dr. Khan's house for two days and these discussions carried on during this time.

It was incumbent upon the Government to call a National Assembly session so that Sheikh Mujibur Rahman could be voted to power. But the men in power in West Pakistan were not in favor of Mujibur Rahman becoming the head of the Government. Mujibur Rahman was not acceptable as the Prime Minister of Pakistan to the *West Pakistani establishment including some political parties* such as the Pakistan People's Party (led by Zulfiqar Ali Bhutto), which stood number two in the elections (81 out of 138 seats in West Pakistan; 0 seats in East Pakistan). As such, President Yahya announced postponement of the National Assembly session scheduled to start in Dacca from March 3, 1971 to a later date.[71]

The postponement of a National Assembly session was based on futile excuses and was done without any valid reason. This advanced the political turmoil in East Pakistan. Sheikh Mujibur Rahman deplored the postponement and called for a hartal (protest/strike) in East Pakistan on March 3.[72] On March 07, 1971, Sheikh Mujibur Rahman, in a speech to a large crowd in Dhaka, called for independence. In East Pakistan, protests were becoming violent and many protesters had picked up arms; West Pakistanis were being killed, harassed, kidnapped or forced to quit East Pakistan.

Meanwhile, Yahya did not come to East Pakistan to assess the ground reality and resolve the issue. The top brass of the army wanted military action and a lot of discussion was taking place. However, Vice-Admiral Syed Mohammad Ahsan was against the use of force, as such he resigned from the Navy. After the resignation of

Vice-Admiral Ahsan as Unified Commander of Eastern Military High Command, on March 07, 1971, AOC Air Commodore Masud was appointed to this position. On March 9, 1971, it was announced that General Tikka Khan would take over as Martial Law Administrator Zone B (with effect from March 7, 1971[73]).

Dr. Akhter Hameed Khan, who was then Vice Chairman and Director of Pakistan (now Bangladesh) Academy Rural Development, was closely watching the actions of the army and the Bengali resentment building against the Pakistan Army. Yahya knew Dr. A.H. Khan's popularity in Bengal and rightly thought Dr. A.H. Khan was the man to speak to in order to understand the ground reality. Thus, Yahya invited Dr. A.H. Khan to come to West Pakistan to meet him. Dr. Khan flew over; however, people who wanted Yahya to be kept ignorant of the ground realities did not let this meeting take place. Dr. Khan was highly perturbed at the way the army was handling the situation.[74]

The President Visits East Pakistan – Air Commodore Masud Speaks Against Use of Force

Given the circumstances, the President was being pressured to visit Dhaka (Dacca) to meet Sheikh Mujibur Rahman to seek a political solution. Yahya, finally under pressure, on March 15, 1971,[75] arrived in Dhaka, the provincial capital of East Pakistan. The next day, i.e., on March 16, 1971 evening, a very important meeting was held at the President's House with senior military officers, Lt. General Tikka Khan, Lt. General S.M.G Peerzada, Major General Aboobaker Osman Mitha, Major General Akbar Khan, Major General Khadim Hussain Raja, Major

General Ghulam Umar, Major General R.F. Ali Khan and Air Commodore Zafar Masud.

AOC Air Cdr. Masud briefed Yahya and the attendees of the conference on the complexity and seriousness of the situation. Air Commodore Masud outspokenly and persuasively told President Yahya:

> "The situation is very delicate. It is essentially a political issue and it needs to be resolved politically, otherwise thousands of innocent men, women and children will perish." Yahya replied "Mitty, I know it... I know it..."[76]

Air Commodore Masud was against the use of force against his own people. His disagreement and antagonism toward the use of force is reiterated by the following sources:

> Air Chief Marshal M. Anwar Shamim wrote in his book, "Lieutenant General Sahibzada Yaqoob Ali Khan, General Officer Commanding East Pakistan and Air Commodore Zafar Masud, Air Officer Commanding East Pakistan gave briefings to the President [Yahya Khan]. They were against taking any large scale action and recommended a political solution to the problem at hand. This was not agreed to by the President."[77]

According to other sources:

> Air Marshal Inam-ul-Haq Khan (Air Commodore in 1971) mentioned in his piece

published in *Defence Journal* (Pakistan): "MZ [Air Commodore M. Zafar Masud] had given a presentation to Yahya [President of Pakistan] and others on 16th March, a copy of which he had sent to Rahim Khan [then Commander-in-Chief of PAF] for approval, prior to the presentation. The conclusion was that military action was not the proper solution to the crisis in East Pakistan. Rahim Khan fully approved the draft and the presentation was made... [Major] General Rao Farman [Ali Khan], on coming out of hall, said to MZ, 'You have said what we could not say.'"[78]

"...'Mitty' Masood were [was] absolutely clear that the situation was such that the army could not possibly control it."[79]

Major General Rao Farman Ali Khan wrote in his book, Air Commodore Masud "...expressed serious concern about the situation and the dangers of a military action."[80]

Muntassir Mamoon mentioned in his book, "...in a meeting between Yahya and other officers, Mitti [Mitty] Masud opposed it, and warned of dire consequences."[81]

Air Cdr. Masud tried to make Yahya and others understand that force would provoke additional violence and build resentment against the Pakistani defense forces. It would also invoke feelings among the masses for separation of East Pakistan from West Pakistan. In short, Air Cdr. Masud's message was that using force against their own people was not the correct strategy and that the best solution was a political dialogue to bring about a settlement. To Air Cdr. Masud, this was the only and the best remedy to end the turmoil. Air Cdr. Masud had reached this solution after closely observing the ground realities in the East wing.[82]

East Pakistan Talks, False Assurances and Military Action Order – Air Commodore Masud Again Warns President

During his stay in Dhaka, Yahya held talks with Mujibur Rahman on March 16 and 17.[83] According Mihir K. Roy, Yahya was assisted by the following individuals: Generals Tikka Khan, Ghulam Umar, Farman Ali Khan, A.O. Mitha, S.M.G Peerzada and Air Commodore Masud. Mujibur Rahman was assisted by Tajudin, Kamal Hossain and Syed Nazural Islam.

The Yahya-Mujibur Rahman meeting seemed to bring fruitful results, and a political accord was most likely achieved; this is evident from a leading Pakistani newspaper's main headline, "Interim Coalition Govt. may be announced tomorrow – Nazrul Islam Likely P.M. [Prime Minister]."[84] Despite this news, Yahya's settlement with Sheikh Mujibur Rahman was not formally announced.

On the same day (March 21, 1971), Bhutto arrived in Dhaka. On March 22, 1971, Yahya had a joint meeting with Bhutto and Mujibur Rahman. Bhutto wanted power for himself and the Pakistani establishment was with him. Yahya and many top officials of the Armed Forces were inclined toward Bhutto, and thus, the meeting brought no solid results. The same day, i.e., on March 22, 1971, postponement of the National Assembly session (which had been re-scheduled to March 25, 1971[85]) was announced. This was reported in *The Pakistan Times*: "National Assembly Session Put Off Again."[86]

This set the stage for further aggravation. Tensions and the separatist movement were so intense that on Pakistan Day (March 23), there was no enthusiasm or celebration in East Pakistan. Instead, the Bengal Students Action Committee observed "Resistance Day." The people were disgusted with the treatment from the Pakistani establishment of the West wing.

On March 24, 1971, an Awami League leader (Tajuddin) speaking to journalists asked the Government to announce the agreed upon terms between Yahya and Mujibur Rahman. *The Pakistan Times* wrote about Tajuddin's demand on its front page headline: "Agreed plan must be announced at once — Delay to be dangerous."[87] But Government failed to move on this demand. As such, the next day, Sheikh Mujibur Rahman (March 25) called for strike to be observed on March 26, 1971.[88]

Yahya took no notice of the strike called by Mujibur Rahman and on the day of the said appeal (i.e. on March 25, 1971), Yahya left for Karachi, West Pakistan, after 11 days of stay in East Pakistan.[89]

Unfortunately, Yahya and the top brass in the Pakistan Army had decided to suppress the Bengalis with the power of the gun. Therefore, *before his departure for Karachi*, Yahya issued orders to launch full-fledged and immediate army action against the Awami League and its Bengali supporters. With this decision, there was no point of return and Pakistan was on its way to break-up.

Air Cdr. Masud was watching the situation with grave concern and felt it was his duty to warn the President once again. At Dhaka airport, when Yahya was leaving for Karachi, Air Cdr. Masud spoke to the President and reminded him of repercussions of using force. *Indeed! Air Commodore Masud displayed extra ordinary moral courage to save the country from ruin.*

Actions in East Pakistan – Air Commodore Masud Faces a Moral Dilemma

On March 26, 1971, Yahya also banned political parties and their activities in Pakistan.[90] "The President, Gen. Agha Mohammad Yahya Khan, today banned all political activities and imposed complete press censorship, throughout Pakistan."[91] Yahya further said, "As for the Awami League, it is completely banned as a political party."[92] Chairman of Pakistan People's Party Zulfiqar Ali Bhutto (who had arrived[93] in Karachi a few hours later than Yahya) supported Yahya's action. Upon arrival, Bhutto told the crowd at the Karachi airport, "By the Grace of Al-mighty God, Pakistan has at last been saved."[94] Bhutto misled the people and on purpose did not tell the nation about ground realities.

Meanwhile, the Martial Law Administrator and Governor of East Pakistan, General Tikka Khan,[95] as per instructions from Yahya, took steps for military action and also promulgated a number of Martial orders to take effect immediately and asked Government servants to report to duty within 24 hours.

On the night of March 25 and 26th, 1971 (at 01 A.M.),[96] the Pakistan Army launched full-scale massive military action known as operation "Searchlight" (a sequel of Operation Blitz launched in November 1970). This was a crackdown on *rebellion Bengali* politicians, civilians, students, professors, and any armed men. The operation began by switching off "…all the civil telephone exchanges at about 2 a.m…action was taken to comb the Dacca University Campus…At 2.30 a.m. the East Pakistan Rifles at Pheelkhana were disarmed…The Reserve Police at Dacca was also disarmed at 3 a.m…"[97] On the morning of March 26, 1971[98], Sheikh Mujibur Rahman was arrested and flown to West Pakistan.

Air Cdr. Masud was expected to support army action and follow orders of bombing the people. *His conscience did not permit him to bomb his own people.* Air Cdr. Masud again tried to reach Yahya several times via phone but the President would not take his phone call. Air Cdr. Masud also flew to West Pakistan and tried to meet Yahya to convey to him that orders of using force must immediately be withdrawn as military action would not succeed. He was right — no war could be won without the support of the people.

Yahya avoided Air Cdr. Masud and was failing to grasp the grave situation — the Government had already lost control in East Pakistan. The President seemed to be unaware of what was happening on the ground, and he failed to comprehend that the vast majority of the Bengalis were supporting Sheikh Mujibur Rahman, the insurgents were taking orders from Mujibur Rahman and the Government in East Pakistan was paralyzed.

Commander-in-Chief of the Pakistan Air Force, Air Marshal Abdur Rahim Khan (who is known to be among the military officers who helped Zulfiqar Ali Bhutto to come to power) asked Air Cdr. Masud to follow orders. Air Cdr Masud was not willing to follow the orders, which is evident from what Air Marshal Inam-ul-Haq wrote in *Defence Journal* (Pakistan):

> "...Tikka retorted, 'Masud, I know that PAF can launch fighters within a couple of minutes. You are dragging your feet and not cooperating since you have been against the military action to start with.'"[99]

The top military brass failed to understand Air Cdr. Masud's perspective and what was coming. The Commander-in-Chief of the Pakistan Air Force, Air Marshal A. Rahim Khan, decided to send Air Commodore (later Air Marshal) Inam-ul-Haq Khan to take charge from Air Cdr. Masud and suppress the Bengalis.

According to the book entitled, *The Story of the Pakistan Air Force — A Saga of Courage and Honour*):

> Air Commodore "Zafar Masud was relieved of his command and told to report to Air Headquarters, where discussions with the C-in-C [Air Marshal A. Rahim Khan] regarding his conduct led to an impasse, and he asked to be released from the PAF. The incident left some in the PAF perplexed about where the line should be drawn between military discipline and higher national interests. Many recognised in Masud's decision the ascendency of high principle over expediency; others saw his conduct downright treasonable."[100]

Air Commodore (later Air Marshal) Inam-ul-Haq Khan who took charge from Air Commodore Zafar Masud wrote in his piece entitled "Saga of PAF in East Pakistan - 1971" in the *Defence Journal* (Pakistan):

> "...The C-in-C gave me a letter addressed to Air Commodore M Z Masud (though known as Mitty Masud but I will call him MZ), Air Officer Commanding, East Pakistan and Base Commander Dacca, asking him to hand over both commands to me immediately as he (MZ) was not in favour of military action and was seen not to be fully cooperating with the Army...

> ...I went to MZ's office and performed the most painful and unpleasant task of handing over the C-in-C's letter. 'Painful and unpleasant' because MZ was and probably, has been, the most brilliant planner and professional commander ever produced by PAF, who very ably led the air battle from Sargodha in the 1965 War. I had the highest regards and respect for him.

> Needless to say that he was shocked and surprised at this unexpected order."[101]

Air Commodore Masud's Resignation

This event in Pakistan's history challenged Air Cdr. Masud on many levels. Ultimately, his personal principles prevailed. He was offered different types of assignments in the Pakistan Air Force; however, he did not take any of the offers and resigned. Air Commodore Masud sacrificed his career and gave away the chance of becoming the

Commander-in-Chief of the PAF (later titled Chief of Air Staff of the Pakistan Air Force).

> Air Chief Marshal Jamal A. Khan wrote: "Spurning other assignments, he [Air Cdr. Masud] preferred to leave the PAF. The air force thus lost one of its finest leaders." [102]

According to *The Story of the Pakistan Air Force — A Saga of Courage and Honour:*

> "...One of the early casualties of that grim 1971 sequence, albeit not in the mortal sense, was Air Commodore Zafar (Mitty) Masud, the Air Officer Commanding the PAF in East Pakistan, who was not only deeply disturbed over the questionable morality of using force to overturn the verdict of an election termed 'fair' by the regime itself; he also had serious misgivings about the military feasibility of the planned operation and had had a rare opportunity to elaborate his arguments against military action to no less a personage than the President of Pakistan [Yahya Khan] in Dhaka in mid March.

> At the end of March, when Operation 'Blitzkrieg' was in full swing, Masud was asked, as he had feared, to mount an air strike against a mob of armed civilians on the outskirts of Dhaka. For Masud it was the worst imaginable moment of truth: should he allow the PAF to participate in what he believed to be a wholly dishonourable operation? On the one hand was his revulsion at the brutality of the proposed strike when viewed against his concept of the justifiable use of military force.

On the other hand was the oath he had taken years before which now demanded his unquestioning obedience. And there was yet another dimension to his inner conflict, not so idealistic: he had by that time clearly demonstrated his eligibility as a future commander of the PAF; taking a firm stand against the authorities now would effectively spell the end of any such prospect. He rejected the strike request.

...As foreseen by a few, 'Blitzkrieg' soon degenerated into a protracted civil war which ended in the dismemberment of Pakistan."[103]

It is widely stated that Yahya should have found a political solution (as Air Cdr. Masud had been recommending) and not taken military action and allowed the National Assembly to elect the Prime Minister of the country. If the assembly had elected Sheikh Mujibur Rahman, then Yahya should have handed over the power to Mujibur Rahman. Many, including those in the Armed Forces of Pakistan, endorse this foresight. Air Chief Marshal Jamal A. Khan wrote in his article:

"Masud later told me that he refused to demand to send combat aircraft to kill rebellious Pakistani citizens armed with spears and sticks because according to his interpretation of military honour an unlawful demand was being made on him. Having studied every detail of the 1970-71 debacle as well as the formally defined norms of professional military ethics in various countries, I remain convinced that Masud was right in refusing to assign his pilots and aircraft to commit an unlawful and dishonourable massacre of civilians. But more than Masud's strong integrity and cold logic, what merits greater recognition is the courage that he brought into play as he dealt with both a moral and personal challenge. I believe he set a very high standard of courage and honour when he made his decision."[104]

The circumstances demonstrate that Air Cdr. Masud was a man of principle and integrity; he could not support a war which was morally wrong. Air Cdr. Masud was a patriot and a great statesman; he stood up for what was best for Pakistan.

After Air Commodore Masud's resignation, the media attempted to reach him for interviews to discuss reasons for his resignation from the Pakistan Air Force and why he ended his bright carrier as the possible future *head of the PAF*; however Air Cdr. Masud was pressured to stay quiet and as usual, the public was deprived of the truth. *Such problems prevail in Pakistan since its creation, and unfortunately it is not realized how much harm keeping vital information hidden inflicts on the country.*

Humiliating Defeat for West Pakistan

In April 1971, Lt. General Amir Abdullah Khan Niazi became Martial Law Administrator Zone B and Commander East Command, Pakistan, replacing General Tikka Khan. Meanwhile, India had intervened and a war between India and Pakistan was taking place over East Pakistan. The Indian Army was helping Mujibur Rahman and the Bengalis to divide Pakistan.

On December 16, 1971, Lt. General Niazi signed the "Instrument of Surrender" and surrendered to the "Joint Command of the Indian and Bangladesh forces" in Dhaka.[105] Pakistan lost its East wing and Bangladesh emerged.

Had President Yahya listened to Air Cdr. Masud, these political issues could have been resolved and Pakistan may have been kept united. With no support from mainstream Bengalis, Pakistani soldiers became demoralized and after nine months of war, Pakistan did not only lose its half (East Pakistan) but underwent a humiliating surrender of 90,000 Pakistanis comprising of civilians and Pakistan defense personnel.

No army can win a war if the public is not supporting it and there is insurgency from within the community against its own armed forces. Now, almost everyone is convinced that military action in Bangladesh was a blunder. Under such circumstances, Air Commodore Masud's refusal to bomb his fellow citizens and to direct the President to seek a political solution was absolutely correct.

Chapter 4: Air Commodore Masud Left His Mark

Air Cdr. Masud's Legacy

Air Commodore Masud was not only a pioneer of the PAF, but throughout his career in PAF, he taught many pilots — many of them emerged as heroes and were given military awards on their outstanding performance. People under his command also rose to high positions including at least two as the head of the PAF (Air Chief Marshal M. Anwar Shamim and Air Chief Marshal Jamal A. Khan).

Air Chief Marshal M. Anwar Shamim in his book wrote:

> "I had the good fortune to serve under him [Air Commodore Masud] four times during my career. I learnt a lot working under him in command as well as in staff appointments."[106]

Air Chief Marshal Jamal A. Khan wrote in his article entitled, "Mitty Masud folds his wings":

> "An exceptional fighter pilot, Masud was at his best when given really challenging assignments, but even when asked to take on some mundane tasks he tackled those with great energy and inventiveness...In 1965, Group Captain Masud became a war hero for his courageous leadership as commander of Pakistan's key air base at Sargodha...

> Masud…was widely respected and regarded as
> a probable future air force chief."[107]

After His Retirement

After his retirement in 1971, Air Commodore Masud
became a professor at the University of Karachi, a well-
known institution in Pakistan. He lectured on war, conflict
resolution and similar topics. Back in 1952, while in the
Pakistan Air Force, Air Cdr. Masud had done his MSc. in
counter-insurgency and he drew upon this knowledge.

Air Commodore Masud was the author/compiler of
highly-praised book, *The Story of the Pakistan Air Force
— A Saga of Courage and Honour*, covering the era 1947-
1988. It was published in 1988 by Shaheen Foundation (a
subsidiary of the Pakistan Air Force) and is an excellent
read for anyone interested in the history of PAF. It is
spread over 700 pages but Air Cdr. Masud did not take
credit for writing such an extensive book. He wrote it as
service to the Pakistan Air Force and to the nation, but
sought no glorification.

Usman Sadiq in his article on Air Commodore Masud
wrote:

> "The book is extremely well detailed and a lot
> of effort must have gone into it. Mitty Sahab
> does not appear to have taken credit for it
> anywhere. I recall writing to the then Air Chief
> about it and got a reply from him saying that
> Mitty Sahab had himself not wanted to take
> credit for this. I don't want to use the word
> modest for him because it isn't the right word.
> I wish I could describe what I mean."[108]

Group Captain (Retd.) S.M. Hali wrote:

> "...'The Story of the Pakistan Air Force' was compiled by Air Commodore M Zafar Masood, euphemistically known as 'Mitty Masood', covering the era 1947-1988..."[109]

M. Zafar Masud Passed Away

Air Commodore Mohammad Zafar Masud passed away on October 07, 2003 in Karachi. He was buried with full military honors at military cemetery in Karachi (Pakistan). Before burial, a contingent of Pakistan Air Force presented him Guard of honor.

Air Commodore Masud will always be remembered as one of the most intelligent and finest officers and a top rated pilot of the Pakistan Air Force. His services to Pakistan and the Pakistan Air Force shall never be forgotten!

May God rest his soul in eternal peace.

Chapter 5: Family Background

Mohammad Zafar Masud was born on October 17, 1927, according to the service record on the Pakistan Air Force and Bharat Rakshak websites.[110]

Air Commodore Mohammad Zafar Masud came from a highly respected and well-educated family. He was the son of Zakia Sultana and her husband. Sultana was the author's mother's first cousin and was one of the nieces of Allama Mashriqi, political theorist, world-famous mathematician, Islamic scholar and the founder of the Khaksar Tehrik (Khaksar Movement), *Al-Islah* newspaper and Islam League.

Zakia Sultana was a well read, cultured and very well-travelled (inside and outside Pakistan) lady. Sultana was wife of Raja Zafar Hussain, Chairman of the Karachi Port Trust and also a Member of the Pakistan Railway Board. Zakia's brother-in-law was Chaudhry Nazir Ahmad, Central Cabinet Minister for Industries from Sept. 1949 to Oct. 1951. Ahmad also held the position of Attorney General of Pakistan. Sultana was regular visitor to the author's house and it is through her that the author and family were kept updated about Air Cdr. Masud's progress in the PAF and other achievements.

Air Cdr. Masud was married to a German lady, Elizabeth Masud. Both had a son, named Mohammed Salar Masud. Air Cdr. Masud's sister, Adeeba Afzal, was married to Brigadier Muhammad Afzal Khan; he was in the Armed Corps of Pakistan Army.

Appendices

1: Photographs

Photo: 1965

Left to right: President Mohammad Ayub Khan and
Group Captain (later Air Commodore) M. Zafar Masud at
PAF Base Sargodha (now PAF Base Mushaf). Masud was
the Base Commander of the said base.

Photo: 1965

Right to left: Group Captain (later Air Commodore) M. Zafar Masud, President Mohammad Ayub Khan, Air Marshal Nur Khan at PAF Base Sargodha (now PAF Base Mushaf). Masud was the Base Commander of the said base.

Photo: 1968

Pakistan Armed Forces Delegation to China.

Air Commodore M. Zafar Masud (front row: extreme
right), Chairman Mao Tse-tung (front row: 5th from
right), General (later President of Pakistan) Agha
Mohammad Yahya Khan (front row: 6th from right),
Premier of China Chou En-lai (front row: 7th from right).

Group Photo of Pakistan Air Force Officers.

M. Asghar Khan (front row: 5th from right) later Air
Marshal, Abdul Rahim Khan (front row: extreme left)
later Air Marshal, Air Commodore M. Zafar Masud
(fourth row: extreme left).

Photo: 1958

Wing Commander (later Air Commodore) M. Zafar
Masud (standing in the front). His team sets a world
record.

W. Cdr. (later Air Commodore) Zafar Masud and his
team sets a World Record.

On February 02, 1958, 16 Sabres of the Pakistan Air
Force under Masud's command went into a loop and
created a precise pattern of a diamond in the sky.

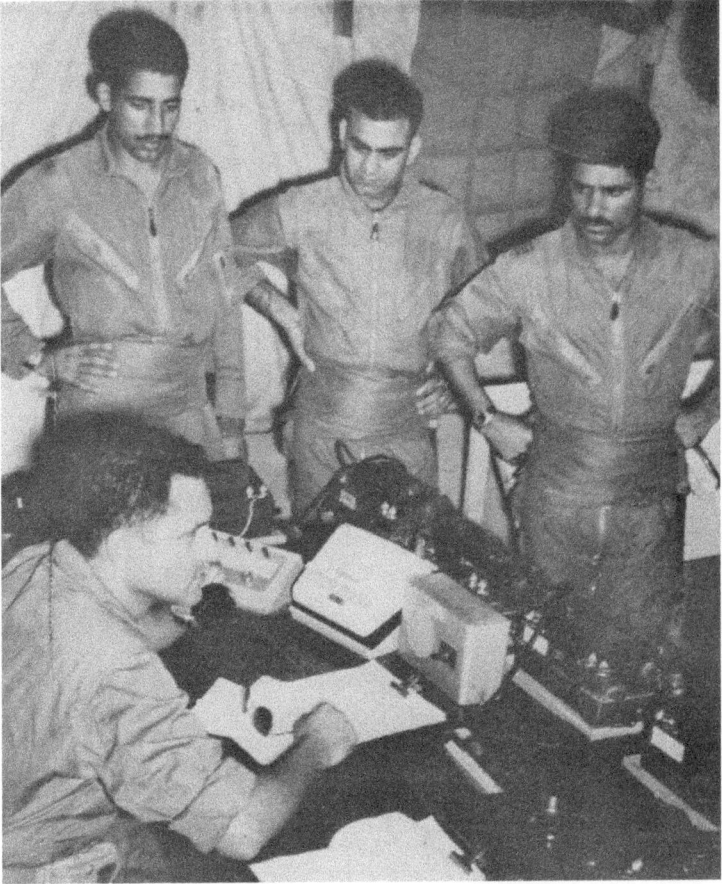

1965 Pakistan-India War.

Base Commander PAF Base Sargodha, Group Captain (later Air Commodore) M. Zafar Masud briefing pilots before the attack on enemy installations/fighter aircrafts.

M. Nur Khan
H.J.

M.Z. Masud
H.J.

S.A. Rafiqui
H.J.

E.G. Hall
S.J.

M.G. Tawab
S.J.

M. Anwar Shamim
S.J.

M.A. Sikander
S.J.

Salahuddin Zahid Butt

Nazir Latif
S.J.

Air Commodore M. Zafar Masud (top center).

Officers of No. 11 Squadron, Drig Road, Karachi (1952).

M. Zafar Masud (sitting 2nd from right) later Air Commodore, Abdul Rahim Khan (sitting 3rd from right) later Air Marshal.

M. Zafar Masud (2nd from right).

M. Zafar Masud (extreme right).

Air Commodore M. Zafar Masud (extreme left), Air
Marshal Abdul Rahim Khan (extreme right).

Group Captain (later Air Commodore) M. Zafar Masud
(left of the table, center), Air Commodore (later Air
Marshal) Abdul Rahim Khan (left of the table, extreme
right).

M. Zafar Masud (extreme left), Abdul Rahim Khan (3rd
from right).

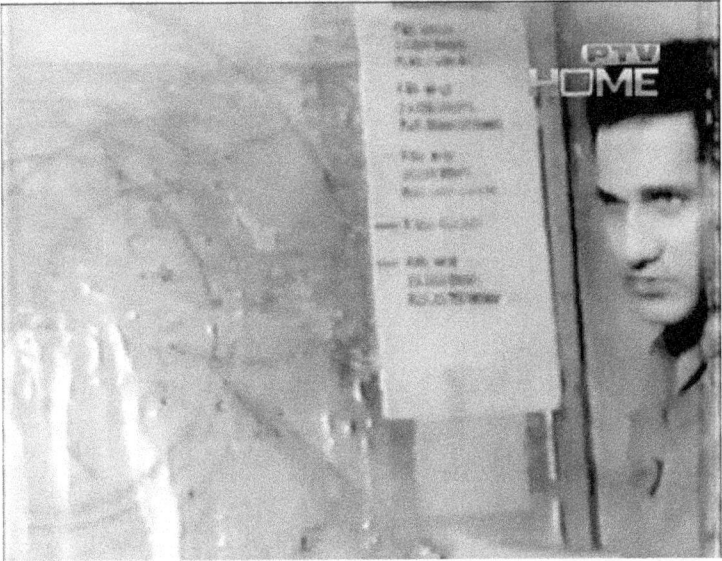

M. Zafar Masud delivering a lecture.

Pilots with Zafar Masud ("Mitty").

2: No. 5 Squadron

On April 12, 1954, Squadron Leader (later Air Commodore) Masud was appointed as the commander of No. 5 Squadron. He remained in this position from April 12, 1954 to February 16, 1955.[111]

The foundation of the said Squadron was actually laid in 1913. On August 15, 1947, a day after the emergence of Pakistan, No. 5 Squadron was established at Peshawar. It started with eight Tempest MK II air crafts. Its first anniversary as a Royal Pakistan Air Force unit was celebrated on July 15, 1948.[112]

On September 21, 1972, No. 5 Squadron was presented with Squadron Color (Flags) for the 1965 and 1971 war operations; the flags were meant to recognize operationally outstanding squadrons.[113]

Syed Shabbir Hussain and M. Tariq Qureshi wrote in their book:

> This unit "…has produced airmen of very high capability, and can rightly take pride in being a squadron of heroes…"[114]

Names (including winners of awards) of No. 5 Squadron can be found in Hussain and Qureshi's book.[115]

3: No. 11 Squadron

This squadron was first established on January 1, 1949 at RPAF Station Mauripur as a light bomber unit.[116] In July 1955, Air Commodore Masud (then Squadron Leader) took over the command of No. 11 Squadron. Then Squadron Leader Masud was the Officer Commanding from July 1955 to August 1957.[117]

This unit became a famous 11 Jet Fighter Squadron. This squadron had the honor to be equipped with first jet aircraft (Attacker). The first three jet planes joined the squadron in August 1951 and with this induction, the Pakistan Air Force entered the jet age. On February 15, 1953, this squadron became first winner of the inter-squadron flight safety trophy. In February 1958, No. 11 Squadron moved from Karachi to Peshawar. In 1965, the squadron was a part of the elite 33 Wing at Sargodha.[118]

For more information, see *The Story of the Pakistan Air Force — A Saga of Courage and Honour*.[119]

4: Major Flaws in Hamoodur Rehman Commission Report

By Nasim Yousaf

The following article appeared in many newspapers:

The Hamoodur Rehman Commission Report (HRCR) is missing many crucial pieces of the puzzle with regards to the factors that led to the division of Pakistan (into Pakistan and Bangladesh) in 1971. A fresh inquiry is needed to fill this major gap.

On December 16, 1971, Bangladesh (formerly East Pakistan) achieved its independence, following a most humiliating surrender by nearly 90,000 soldiers of the Pakistan Armed Forces. Ten days after the emergence of Bangladesh, the Government of Pakistan (through notification Number: SRO [I] 71, dated December 26, 1971) appointed the Hamoodur Rehman Commission to investigate the events leading up to the surrender of the armed forces of Pakistan in East Pakistan and the ceasefire on the borders of West Pakistan. The Commission was comprised of three senior judges: Chief Justice of the Supreme Court Hamoodur Rehman, Chief Justice of the Lahore High Court Anwarul Haq, and Chief Justice of the Sind and Baluchistan High Court Justice Tufail Ali Abdul Rehman Zubedi. However, when the Commission completed its inquiry, the final report was promptly shelved in order to keep its findings hidden.

In August of 2000, extracts from the Commission's final report were leaked and published by "India Today." Thereafter, the HRC report was printed in book form by a Pakistani publisher under the title *The Report of the Hamoodur Rehman Commission of Inquiry into the 1971 War [Declassified by the Government of Pakistan]*. As per the contents of this book, the original HRC report had "4000 typed pages" and "374 exhibits." However, the published version of the report included only 545 pages (the full version does not appear to have been published).

I am currently doing research on the late Air Commodore M. Zafar Masud (recipient of the *Hilal-e-Jurat* and *Sitara-e-Basalat* awards), who was the Air Officer Commanding, East Pakistan (1970-1971), and considered to be the future Chief of Staff of the Pakistan Air Force. I have reviewed the published (545 page) Hamoodur Rehman Commission Report (HRCR) and found that the HRCR has many inadequacies. More specifically, below are some major items that were excluded from the report:

1) Air Commodore Masud's briefing to the late President of Pakistan, General Agha Mohammad Yahya Khan, at a conference held on March 16, 1971 in Dhaka (a copy of this briefing was also sent to then Commander-in-Chief of the Pakistani Air Force, Air Marshal Abdur Rahim Khan). This conference, attended by many Army Generals, took place *only ten days* prior to the military action in East Pakistan.

2) Details of Air Commodore Masud's resignation and his dispute with the President of Pakistan and Air Marshal Rahim Khan over the use of force (Commodore Masud sacrificed his bright military

career to try and save the country from breaking up).

3) A recorded interview of Air Commodore Masud by the Hamoodur Rehman Commission. The commission recorded interviews with members of the armed forces. However, Air Commodore Masud's statement is not included in the HRCR interviews that were released. It is unknown whether Air Commodore Masud's statement was recorded and omitted from the published report or if it was not recorded at all. If it was not recorded, then one must question why the Commission did not document such an important point of view (Air Commodore Masud was still alive when the HRCR was prepared; he died in 2003).

In addition to the omission of vital details regarding Air Commodore Masud, the HRCR also ignores crucial mistakes by Pakistan's founding fathers and the Pakistani establishment in the years leading up to the division of the country in 1971. Key pieces of information overlooked by the report in this regard include:

1) The intolerance and suppression of opposition leaders (including Allama Mashriqi in West Pakistan and Maulana Bhashani in East Pakistan) from 1947 onwards. This type of treatment destroyed democracy from the very birth of Pakistan.

2) Allama Mashriqi's warning regarding the break-up of Pakistan during his speech at a public meeting at Iqbal Park (Lahore) in 1956. Mashriqi stated, *"Ye Muslims! Today from this platform I sound you a warning...In 1970 — I see it clearly*

— the nation will be stormed from all sides. The internal situation would have deteriorated gravely. A panic of widespread bloodshed will sweep the nation. The frenzy of racial and provincial prejudices will grip the whole country. Zindabad and murdabad will defean your ears. Plans will be initiated to dismember the country. Take it from me that in 1970, Pakistan will be plagued with a grave threat to its sovereignty. You might actually lose it if the reigns of the country were not in the hands of courageous and unrelenting leadership." This forewarning was based on the mishandling of political affairs in the East wing.

3) Mashriqi's various suggestions to the top leadership of Pakistan to keep the two wings of Pakistan united.

4) The Bengalis' resentment of Quaid-e-Azam Mohammad Ali Jinnah (Founder of Pakistan) as a result of disagreements over issues such as his failure to accept Bengali as a national language (see Jinnah's speech in Dhaka on March 21, 1948).

5) The discrimination against East Pakistan that led to the total collapse of Jinnah's Muslim League in the first provincial elections held in 1954 in East Pakistan.

Given these gross oversights, it seems that the true intention of the HRCR was not to actually study the circumstances that led to the debacle of East Pakistan; rather, it was to shift blame away from the political leadership and toward other groups, including the Armed Forces, India, and the Hindus of East Pakistan. In doing so, the report completely overlooked the most unfortunate actions of the Pakistani political leadership and the establishment from the time that the country was formed in 1947. It is clear that the HRC report, as it stands, is *incomplete* and cannot be viewed as an objective account of the reasons for the break-up of the country in 1971.

The recent general elections provide some hope for a new Pakistan. But a new Pakistan requires a fundamental rethinking of every major institution in the country and a correction of the nation's flawed educational syllabus and concocted history books. This massive overhaul can take place only when the masses are provided with *unbiased* knowledge of the nation's history, the mistakes of its founding fathers, the opposing views of Jinnah's contemporaries (including Allama Mashriqi), and how the country's democratic institutions were eroded from the very outset. Therefore, the new Government must reopen the inquiry and appoint a new commission to look into the break-up of the nation in 1971. It should empower this commission to write openly without reservation and examine all issues comprehensively (including the points mentioned in this article), from 1947 to 1971. This new report would enable the nation to turn the page on a deplorable and depressing period in its history and serve as an extremely important step towards avoiding another break-up of the nation.

*****

This piece was published in the following:

- *The Lahore Times*, May 20, 2013
- *The Eastern Post*, June 05, 2013, Vol. 6. No. 44
- *Cutting Edge*, May 23-29, 2013, p. 09
- *OYE! Times* (USA), May 17, 2013

- *Paktoonistan Gazette*, June 03, 2013
- *PK Articles hub*, June 02, 2013
- *Paigham*
- *Allvoices* (USA), May 18, 2013
- *Pakistan Defence* web site, May 24, 2013
- *Make Pakistan Better*, May 21, 2013

5: What Led to the Separation of East Pakistan and Emergence of Bangladesh?

By Nasim Yousaf

Once a freedom movement penetrates the masses, it cannot be controlled by the power of the gun. Allama Mashriqi's Khaksar Movement in British India is just one example. Based on ground realities, the Pakistani military commanders failed to comprehend that the only way they could have saved East Pakistan from breaking away was through justice and a political settlement.

***

When re-visiting the events surrounding the history of Pakistan, one can easily ascertain that the war of liberation for Bangladesh actually began right after the emergence of Pakistan in 1947. In addition to the expected challenges associated with a geographically split country (India lay in the middle of East and West Pakistan), resentment in East Pakistan began to grow as West Pakistan seemed to dominate in all spheres. From the start, resources and investment were mainly directed toward the West. The Bengalis felt marginalized and developed a bitterness toward Quaid-e-Azam Muhammad Ali Jinnah, the founder of Pakistan, the Muslim League (after the partition of India the All-India Muslim League, AIML, was called Muslim League), and the West Pakistani *establishment* (influential persons or those in power).

A number of events led to this. For example, soon after the creation of Pakistan, Jinnah rejected the Bengali people's (who were in majority in Pakistan) demand and made it clear to them that their Bengali language would not be accepted as a national/official language.

> On March 21, 1948, in a speech at Dhaka, Jinnah stated: "…let me make it very clear to you that the State language of Pakistan is going to be Urdu and no other language…"[120]

This speech highly offended the people of the East Pakistan. To Bengalis, who were the majority in Pakistan, it was their legitimate right to have Bengali recognized at the national level. They also expected Jinnah to make Dhaka the capital of the country versus Karachi. Both expectations were not met.

Jinnah also did not realize that many Bengalis held resentment against him from before partition over the mistreatment of A. K. Fazlul Haq (a prominent Bengali politician and member of the AIML) who had presented the Lahore Resolution (Pakistan Resolution) in March 1940 at the All-India Muslim League session at Lahore. Haq did not appreciate Jinnah's dictatorial and authoritarian style; this led to the deterioration of their relationship. Jinnah expelled him from the AIML and asked him to resign, which he did in 1941. Haq also resigned from the National Defence Council.

> According to the newspaper, "Huq stated…principles of democracy and autonomy in the All-India Muslim League were being subordinated 'to the arbitrary wishes of a single individual [Quaid-e-Azam], who seeks

to rule as an omnipotent authority even over
the destiny of thirty-three millions of Muslims
in the province of Bengal, who occupy the key
position in Indian Muslim politics."'[121]

Moreover, Jinnah did not visit Bengal when riots broke
out in 1946 (after Jinnah called for "Direct Action") and
large numbers of Bengalis were butchered in Calcutta and
other parts of Bengal.

Such circumstances since before and after partition and
the discriminatory policies against East Pakistanis led to a
deep aversion among the Bengalis against the Muslim
League and its leadership.[122] As such, in the first general
election in East Pakistan (1954), the Muslim League was
wiped out. Thereafter, the Muslim League completely
collapsed in Pakistan; the factions that emerged later on
and now exist in the country are not related to the *original*
or Jinnah's Muslim League (formed by the upper-class of
Muslims in 1906).

***

Meanwhile, Allama Mashriqi (founder of the Khaksar
Tehrik movement, a leading force in attaining
independence of the Indian subcontinent from colonial
British rule in 1947) had been stating to Pakistani men in
power not to make discriminatory policies. He made
multiple suggestions to the Government in order to form a
bond between East and West Pakistanis. These included
(among others):

- Give due share to Bengalis in terms of positions in
  senior administration and policy making

- Ensure justice in the distribution of funds and other assets
- Invest equally in industrial projects
- Promote social exchange, for example, provide incentives to encourage Bengalis to move to West Pakistan and vice versa and encourage via incentives inter-marriages between Bengalis and non-Bengalis

The Pakistani *establishment* could not comprehend Mashriqi's vision (just as they had not understood his vision when he opposed the division of India). They kept ignoring ground realities and over the years, the situation kept worsening.

Therefore, in 1956, in front of a very large gathering at Minto Park (later Iqbal Park), Lahore, Mashriqi issued the following momentous warning:

> "Ye Muslims! Today from this platform I sound you a warning. Listen carefully and ponder. Sometime in the future, probably in 1970, you will be confronted with a perilous situation. In 1970—I see it clearly—the nation will be stormed from all sides. The internal situation would have deteriorated gravely. A panic of widespread bloodshed will sweep the nation. The frenzy of racial and provincial prejudices will grip the whole country. Zindabad and murdabad will defean your ears. Plans will be initiated to dismember the country. Take it from me that in 1970, Pakistan will be plagued with a grave threat to its sovereignty. You might actually lose it if the reigns of the country were not in the hands of courageous and unrelenting leadership.

India will, in that grave situation, try to take advantage of your internal turmoil and devour you. Or, the governance of the country will fall in the hands of spineless self-seekers or self-centred opportunists who might on their own accord push you into the Indian lap. I warn you about 1970. I warn you to prepare from now to face the situation which will emerge in that year."[123]

It is incredible that Allama Mashriqi made this warning in the 1950s – so far ahead of time – it was based on the handling of affairs in East Pakistan and the treatment of Bengalis.

***

Fast forwarding ahead to the 1970s, on December 07, 1970, for the first time in the history of Pakistan, free and fair general elections were held under President of Pakistan, Agha Mohammad Yahya Khan. The Awami League of Sheikh Mujibur Rahman won 160 out of the 162 seats allotted for East Pakistan. The majority of the seats in the National Assembly went to the Awami League. The Pakistan People's Party (PPP) of Zulfiqar Ali Bhutto won 81 seats out of 138 seats in West Pakistan (0 seats in East Pakistan). With a clear victory of the Awami League in East Pakistan, Sheikh Mujibur Rahman was well-positioned to become the next Prime Minister of Pakistan, provided he would be voted to the position in the National Assembly.

However, the National Assembly session was postponed on March 1, 1971[124] in order to prevent the National Assembly from electing Mujibur Rahman to the said post.

This was mainly sabotaged by Bhutto and the West Pakistani *establishment* (which included politicians, senior bureaucrats of the civil administration, top brass of the Armed Forces, and top level businessmen).

This postponement led Mujibur Rahman to declare an open revolt to seek public support for an independent Bangladesh. Mujibur Rahman made a public address on March 07, 1971: "This struggle is the struggle for freedom, this struggle is the struggle for independence."[125] Thus, civil disobedience and a movement to paralyze the government began. Then, he issued the following directive until his demands were met:

> "1. No tax campaign to continue.
>
> 2. The Secretariat, government and semi-government offices, high courts, and other courts throughout Bangladesh should observe hartals [strikes]. Appropriate exemptions shall be announced from time to time.
>
> 3. Railway and ports may function but railway workers and port workers should not cooperate if railways or ports are used for mobilization of forces for the purpose of carrying out repression against the people.
>
> 4. Radio, television and newspapers shall give complete versions of our statements and shall not suppress news about the people's movement otherwise Bengalis working in these establishments shall not cooperate.
>
> 5. Only local and inter-district trunk telephones communication shall function.
>
> 6. All educational institutions shall remain closed.

7. Banks shall not effect remittances to the Western Wing either through the State Bank or otherwise.

8. Black flags shall be hoisted on all buildings every day.

9. Hartal is withdrawn in all other spheres but complete hartal may be declared at any moment depending upon the situation.

10. A Sanram Parishad should be organised in each union, *mohallah*, *thana*, sub-division and district under the leadership of the local Awami League units." [126]

By this order, Mujibur Rahman began gathering power in his hands and at the same time conveyed to everyone that no solution short of transferring power to him was acceptable. On March 23 (Pakistan Day), instead of the Pakistani flag, a "…new flag of Bangladesh appeared on government buildings and private houses and Shaikh Mujibur Rahman himself hoisted the Bangladesh flag on his residence."[127]

***

No fruitful progress or settlement was reached between Mujibur Rahman, Yahya and Bhutto. Mujibur Rahman continued to increase his grip over the provincial government; the central government had almost collapsed in East Pakistan. According to Hamoodur Rehman Commission's report (see end note and later part of this work for description of this report): "…from the 1st of March to the 25th March 1971, the Awami League had taken complete control of East Pakistan, paralysing the authority of the federal government."[128]

In addition, respected individuals, including Air Commodore M. Zafar Masud, were warning the President of the situation. However, President Yahya failed to realize not only the extent of the escalating situation but also the following factors that were illuminating the dangerous situation:

- The bulk of the Pakistani Armed Forces were in West Pakistan and could not be moved to East Pakistan for various reasons
- Some external powers, mainly India, were helping the separatist movement in order to dismember Pakistan
- The Pakistan Air Force was very weak in comparison to India and the strength of the Indian Armed forces had grown (was much better in 1971 than in 1965)
- Pakistan was incapable of fighting a war on two fronts, i.e. with the local people in East Pakistan and with India
- The West Pakistani Army was not trained to fight on East Pakistan's terrain
- The Bengali people had become hostile and no war can be won without public support
- World opinion was forming with the suppressed Bengali people

According to Hamoodur Rehman Commission Report:

"...we have not been able to find upon the evidence that there was any proper concept of manpower planning either within the armed services or at the national level. It is remarkable that, even in the critical months after March, 1971 when war was clearly a probability, if not an imminent certainly, the question seems to have bothered the general staff very little. It does not appear that even the chief of staff, much less then the commander-in-chief, ever showed any interest in this all-important question."[129]

Unfortunately, the paralysis of the government in the East Wing and warnings from respected persons did not wake up the President, civil administration and leaders, and political parties of West Pakistan.

***

With the support of the Pakistan People's Party, Jamaat-e-Islami[130], and others, President Yahya ordered to suppress the Bengali uprise with force.

Based on the Army's actions against students, politicians, and others, including disarming of forces such as the East Pakistan Rifles, Reserve Police at Dhaka, and East Bengal Regiment,[131] even the Bengalis who had supported the military turned against the Pakistani Armed Forces. The Bengalis' hatred and determination to seek independence grew and they were no longer scared of Pakistan defense forces; in fact it was the other way around. The circumstances confirm that Yahya underestimated the strength and determination of Bengalis to fight the Pakistan Armed Forces. With the Bengalis' rise, many in the Pakistan Armed Forces lost the will to fight and did not consider this war against their own brothers to be legitimate.

Furthermore, many Bengalis fled to India; this and the Pakistan Army's actions opened the door for India and Mukti Bahini guerillas (armed Bengali insurgents) to seek world opinion in their favor and for the emergence of Bangladesh.

On the "night of the 20th and 21st November 1971, the Indian Army openly launched an attack..."[132] With India entering, Pakistan's forces had to fight with Bengalis *and* the Indian Army. Meanwhile, the President and some Generals (including the one in East Pakistan) were honeymooning with females during one of the most crucial period in Pakistan's history.[133]

Pakistan suffered a humiliating defeat in the war and 90,000 members of the Pakistan Army surrendered on December 16, 1971 to the Indian army.[134]

***

Many sad reflections emerge from this time in the nation's history – from the atrocities that took place during the war to the politics in the country.

During the uprise in Bangladesh, the Pakistan Army committed atrocities on innocent Bengalis. Similarly, the Awami League militants were brutal toward pro-Pakistani people. Both sides acted under the influence of anger and revenge and committed extensive and senseless acts, such as killing, rape, looting, abduction, burning of homes, physical torture, and burying of people in mass graves.

After the emergence of Bangladesh, Mukti Bahini went after non-Bengalis and undertook wholesale slaughter of West Pakistani families, whether they favored military action or not. They inflicted such implausible cruelty which is rarely seen in history. This was done despite the promise by the Chief of Staff of the Indian Army and the terms of surrender that no revenge activity would take place. According to Hamoodur Rehman Report: "Harrowing tales of these atrocities were narrated by the large number of West Pakistanis and Biharis who were able to escape..."[135]

If one hears the Bangladeshi side of the story about the Pakistan Army's brutality, it is equally horrifying and accounts include killing of Bengali professionals, businessmen, industrialists, civilians and those of Hindu religion, destruction of rails, roads, bridges and vital installations, and raping of females by men of the Armed Forces. There is a large list of cruelties committed by the Pakistan Armed Forces.

This senseless cruelty on both sides represents a sad chapter in the history of the region. Moreover, the politics of the time are also beyond disappointing, to say the least. For instance, shortly before the surrender, Bhutto had joined the government as the Deputy Prime Minister. In this capacity, he went to USA. At a United Nations Security Council meeting, he stormed out and tore into pieces the resolution put forth to end the fighting; he declared a 'thousands years war' with India. He did this on purpose, keeping in view the emotional psyche of his people. He succeeded in getting admiration for this action. It is a dilemma that people of Pakistan do not understand such moves of Pakistani politicians and that is why they have been suffering under different leaders since 1947.

After the war, the Government of Pakistan established a Commission headed by Chief Justice of Supreme Court of Pakistan called Hamoodur Rehman Commission (HRC). It is known that originally there was more than one copy of the preliminary HRC report. However, to conceal the facts, these were all destroyed, except the one that was handed over to the then Prime Minister Zulfiqar Ali Bhutto. Upon return of the Pakistan prisoners of war (POWs) from India, HRC recorded additional statements and gave its final report to the authorities in 1974. Unfortunately, this report was not made public for a long time until some parts of it were leaked and published in India in year 2000. This obviously put tremendous pressure on the Pakistani Government; therefore the report was finally published in the same year.

Ironically, this published report does not include Air Commodore Masud's (Air Officer Commanding in East Pakistan in 1971) briefing to Yahya on March 16, 1971 and his discussions with the military brass are also excluded from HRC. It is unknown whether HRC had invited him to record his statement. The absence of his statement and discussions is a blunder on the part of the Hamoodur Rehman Commission and makes the quality of report dubious.[136]

***

Finally, the blame game is always played when people reflect on this war. Many people blame India for the separation of East Pakistan. A section of people also think that India wanted to amalgamate East Pakistan. Indeed, it was in the strategic interest of India to see East Pakistan separated but to place the entire blame on India does not make sense based on the circumstances of the time as have been explained in this work. India was overall satisfied with the portion of the country they received in 1947.

Some also shift blame on the late President Mohammad Ayub Khan. This again is misinformed; the Green Revolution in Bangladesh was achieved by Dr. Akhtar Hameed Khan during Ayub Khan's tenure. Ayub supported Dr. A. H. Khan wholeheartedly, and this demonstrates that Ayub Khan was in support of development and progress in Bangladesh.

The matter of fact is that since 1947, the Pakistani leadership had been incapable of making Bengalis feel part of the community. If the leadership of Pakistan had treated Bengalis on equal footing right from 1947 through the elections of the 1970s and had redressed Bengali grievances, uprise amongst Bengalis would not have taken place and India would not have had the opportunity to intervene or influence world opinion.

Sadly, Pakistan still has not learned hard but valuable lessons from the time of partition to the separation of East Pakistan to today's prevailing poor circumstances. If Allama Mashriqi and Air Commodore Masud's words of caution were followed, Pakistan would not have lost East Pakistan.

6: Index

7: References

[1] *Hilal-e-Jurat* is the Crescent of Courage; it is the second highest military award of Pakistan. *Sitara-e-Basalat* is given to individuals for distinguished and exceptional acts of gallantry, valor or courage while performing their duty.

[2] Facebook Page Air Commodore Masud: https://www.facebook.com/AirCommodoreMZafarMasud

[3] Khan, Air Chief Marshal Jamal A. "Mitty Masud folds his wings." *Dawn*, Karachi, Pakistan. October 13, 2003. http://www.dawn.com/news/1065137. Last accessed November, 2014.

[4] Khan, Air Marshal (Retd.) Inam-ul-Haq. "Saga of PAF in East Pakistan – 1971." *Defence Journal*, Karachi, Pakistan. Vol. 12, Issue 10, May 2009, p. 42. (Also spelled as Inam-ul-Haque Khan.)

[5] Khan, Air Marshal (Retd.) Ayaz Ahmed. "Past Present And Future: Pakistan Air Force." *Globe* magazine, Pakistan. Vol. 4, September 1991, p. 89.

[6] Sadiq, Usman. "Air Commodore Mitty Masud; As I Knew Him." *PakDef Military Consortium*. http://pakdef.org/air-commodore-mitty-masud-as-i-knew-him/. Last accessed November, 2014.

[7] "Former air commodore Mitty Masud dies." *Daily Times*, Lahore, Pakistan. October 8, 2003. http://archives.dailytimes.com.pk/national/08-Oct-2003/former-air-commodore-mitty-masud-dies. Last accessed November, 2014.

[8] "Battle Lines of the PAF. PAF Base Sargodha History: 1948-1988." *PAF Falcons* website. http://www.paffalcons.com/bases/sargodha-1948-1988.php. Last accessed November, 2014.

[9] Masud is also spelled Masood.

[10] Hussain, Syed Shabbir and Squadron Leader M. Tariq Qureshi. *History of the Pakistan Air Force (1947-1982)* First Edition. Masroor, Karachi: Pakistan Air Force press, 1982, p. 5.

[11] Masud, Air Commodore Zafar. *The Story of the Pakistan Air Force — A Saga of Courage and Honour*. Islamabad, Pakistan: Shaheen Foundation, 1988, p. 23.

This book was commissioned by Air Chief Marshal Jamal A. Khan (*The Nation*, March 25, 2009). According to a book entitled, *The Story of the Pakistan Air Force — 1988-1998: A Battle Against Odds*: "Air Marshal Jamal A. Khan was closely associated with the first volume of 'The Story of the Pakistan Air Force'. He contributed one chapter [no chapter name provided] to the book and his efforts culminated in the publication of the volume in 1988, under the supervision of Air Commodore M. Zafar Masud." (Shaikh, A. Rashid. *The Story of the Pakistan Air Force — 1988-1998: A Battle Against Odds*. Islamabad, Pakistan: Shaheen Foundation, produced by Oxford University Press, 2000, p. 351.)

See Chapter 4 within this book for more information.

[12] Hussain and Qureshi, p. 10.

[13] Ibid.

[14] "History of PAF." *Pakistan Air Force* website. http://paf.gov.pk/history.html. Last accessed December, 2014.

[15] Hussain and Qureshi, p. 5.

[16] Masud, p. 63.

[17] The Royal Indian Air Force personnel had been working together as a team and many pilots had undergone the same training and had served in the same squadrons during World War II. It is sad that at the time of partition, they became die-hard enemies and not only fought for the distribution of Royal Indian Air Force possessions but also over control of Kashmir.

[18] *The Pakistan Times*, Lahore, Pakistan, June 13, 1947.

[19] *The Pakistan Times*, Lahore, Pakistan, July 13, 1947.

[20] "History of PAF." *Pakistan Air Force* website. http://www.paf.gov.pk/history.html. Last accessed November, 2014.

[21] Masud, p. 63.

[22] Hussain and Qureshi, p. 27.

[23] According to a magazine based in the United Kingdom, *The Aeroplane*, "When Pakistan came into being as a nation, two of the 10 squadrons then comprising the I.A.F. were allotted to it, together with 44 pilots, 2,000 airmen and about 200 officers. None of its aircraft was serviceable, with the exception of one Dakota, and the operational establishment comprised a handful of Tempests." ("The Pakistan Air Force." *The Aeroplane*, Temple Press Limited, U.K. Vol. XCIV, No. 2425, February 21, 1958, p. 247.)

[24] Masud, p. 16.

[25] Masud, pp. 15-17.

[26] "History of PAF: Pioneering Officers." *Pakistan Air Force* website. http://www.paf.gov.pk/pioneering_officers.html. Last accessed November, 2014.

[27] "Life in Pakistan Air Force." *Pakistan Air Force* website. http://www.paf.gov.pk/record_sec.html.

Last accessed November, 2014.

[28] "History of PAF: Pioneering Officers." *Pakistan Air Force* website. http://www.paf.gov.pk/pioneering_officers.html. Last accessed November, 2014.

[29] Masud, p. 222.

[30] Ibid.

[31] According to *The International News* (Pakistan), October 23, 2013: "Pakistan and the US have had a volatile relationship during the last sixty-six years, which saw the flow of US

assistance periodically interrupted, yet US during the last 64 years (1948-2012) provided $68 billion in aid and assistance to Pakistan, which included $42 billion in economic aid, while the remaining $26 billion in military assistance." ("Pakistan received $68 billion in US assistance during 66 years." *The International News*, Pakistan. October 23, 2013. http://www.thenews.com.pk/article-123489-Pakistan-received-$68-billion-in-US-assistance-during-66-years. Last accessed November, 2014.)

[32] Masud, p. 56.

[33] "The Pakistan Air Force." *The Aeroplane*, p. 247.

[34] "Far-away Frontiers." *The Aeroplane*, Temple Press Limited, U.K. Vol. XCIV, No. 2426, February 28, 1958, p. 285.

[35] *International News Network.* http://www.onlinenews.com.pk/details.php?id=40190. Last accessed March, 2011.

[36] Khan, Air Chief Marshal Jamal A. *Dawn*, October 13, 2003.

[37] "Air Commodore Mohammad Zafar Masud." *Indian Bharat Rakshak* website. http://www.bharat-rakshak.com/IAF/Database/Record/view.php?srnum=3314. Last accessed November, 2014.

[38] Khan, Air Chief Marshal Jamal A. *Dawn*, October 13, 2003.

[39] Shamim, Air Chief Marshal (Retd.) M. Anwar. *Cutting Edge PAF.* Pakistan: Vanguard Books Pvt. Ltd., 2010, p. 63.

[40] Masud, p. 491.

[41] Hussain and Qureshi, p. 108.

[42] Hussain and Qureshi, p. 107.

[43] Masud, p. 69.

[44] "Pakistan Shows its Sabres." *The Aeroplane*, Temple Press Limited, U.K. Vol. XCIV, No. 2424, February 14, 1958, p. 208.

[45] "Pakistan Shows its Sabres." *The Aeroplane*, p. 209. Also see photos of the formation in "The Pakistan Air Force." *The Aeroplane*, pp. 227, 248.

[46] Khan, Air Chief Marshal Jamal A. *Dawn*, October 13, 2003.

[47] Masud, p. 684.

[48] *Global Security.org.* http://www.globalsecurity.org/military/world/pakistan/sargodh a-ab.htm. Last accessed November, 2014. ("GlobalSecurity.org is the leading source of background information and developing news stories in the fields of defense, space, intelligence, WMD, and homeland security.")

[49] "Pakistan's 'Top Gun' Base." *PakDef Military Consortium.* http://pakdef.org/pakistans-top-gun-base/. Last accessed November, 2014.

[50] Khan, Air Chief Marshal Jamal A. *Dawn*, October 13, 2003.

[51] PAF Base Sargodha (now PAF Base Mushaf) is one of the most important bases of the Pakistan Air Force. It is located at Sargodha in the Punjab province of Pakistan. It is the headquarters of the PAF Central Air Command. Its importance from early on is well-known; Sargodha initially hosted all the new types of aircrafts which were procured by the Air Force, for example the F-6, F-16, F-86, F-104, and Mirage.

[52] Hussain and Qureshi, p. 76.

[53] Ibid.

[54] Khan, Mohammad Ayub and Rais Ahmad Jafri (editor). *Ayub, Soldier and Statesman: Speeches and Statements (1958-1965) of Field Marshal Mohammad Ayub Khan, President of Pakistan & A Detailed Account of the Indo-Pakistan War (1965).* Lahore, Pakistan: Mohammad Ali Academy, 1966, p. 400.

[55] Masud, p. 73.

[56] *The News* Daily, Pakistan, March 18, 2013.

[57] The Star of Courage.

[58] Hussain and Qureshi, p. 47.

[59] Khan, Air Marshal (Retd.) Ayaz Ahmed. *Globe*, September 1991, p. 90.

[60] Khan, Mohammad Ayub and Jafri, p. 400.

[61] Hussain and Qureshi, p. 227.

[62] Rufus, Wing Commander (Retd.) RA. "Flying the AN-12: The AN-12 in the Bombing Role – 2." *Indian Bharat Rakshak* website. http://www.bharat-rakshak.com/IAF/History/1965War/An-12s-2.html. Last accessed November, 2014.

[63] Khan, Mohammad Ayub and Jafri, p. 159.

[64] Hussain and Qureshi, p. 227.

[65] *Daily Times*, Lahore, Pakistan, October 8, 2003.

[66] Khan, Mohammad Ayub and Jafri, p. 400.

[67] The list of officers published in *Pakistan Review* who received *Hilal-e-Jurat* included four Major Generals, five Brigadiers and Group Captain M. Zafar Masud. (Haye, A. Qadir. "Gallery of National Heroes." *Pakistan Review*. Vol. 13, December 1965, pp. 32-33.)

[68] Masud, p. 671.

[69] "Chairman Mao Receives Pakistan Armed Forces Goodwill Delegation." *Peking Review*. Vol. 46, November 15, 1968, pp. 3-4.

[70] *Dawn*, Karachi, Pakistan, October 13, 2003.

[71] *Dawn*, Karachi, Pakistan, March 2, 1971.

[72] Ibid.

[73] *Dawn*, Karachi, Pakistan, March 10, 1971.

[74] Dr. A.H. Khan was in Comilla until April 11, 1971 and saw the army action start on March 25, 1971.

[75] *Dawn*, Karachi, Pakistan, March 16, 1971.

[76] Salik, Siddiq. *Witness To Surrender*. Pakistan: Oxford University Press, 1977, p. 61.

[77] Shamim, p. 179.

[78] Khan, Air Marshal (Retd.) Inam-ul-Haq. *Defence Journal*, May 2009.

[79] Mitha, Aboobaker Osman. *Unlikely Beginnings: A Soldier's Life*. Karachi, Pakistan: Oxford University Press, 2003, p. 334.

[80] Khan, Major General Rao Farman Ali. *How Pakistan Got Divided*. Lahore, Pakistan: Jang Publishers, 1992, p. 74.

[81] Mamoon, Muntassir. *The Vanquished Generals and the Liberation War of Bangladesh*. Somoy Prokashan, 2000, p. 66.

[82] I have been a Pilot Officer in the Pakistan Air Force and am a son of an Army Officer; as such I am familiar with defense officers' lifestyle and way of thinking. The problem with the Armed Forces officers is that they are not encouraged to meet civilians. They lead their lives in Officer Messes or Cantonements, as such they cannot comprehend ground realities. Under these circumstances, for Yahya to realize the public mood was inconceivable. He thought he could arrest Mujibur Rahman and silence the public with the power of the cannon.

[83] *Dawn*, Karachi, Pakistan, March 17-18, 1971.

[84] *The Pakistan Times*, Lahore, Pakistan, March 22, 1971.

[85] *The Pakistan Times*, Lahore, Pakistan, March 07, 1971.

[86] *The Pakistan Times*, Lahore, Pakistan, March 23, 1971.

[87] *The Pakistan Times*, Lahore, Pakistan, March 25, 1971.

[88] *The Pakistan Times*, Lahore, Pakistan, March 26, 1971.

[89] Ibid.

[90] At the time, I was a college student and was reading about the developments on a daily basis. I felt that the Government was doing injustice to the Awami League.

[91] *Dawn*, Karachi, Pakistan, March 27, 1971. Also see *The Pakistan Times*, Lahore, Pakistan, March 27, 1971.

[92] *Dawn*, Karachi, Pakistan, March 27, 1971.

[93] The following persons also returned with Bhutto: Hafiz Peerzada, Ghulam Mustafa Khar, Mirza Rafi Raza, Ali Ahmed Khan Talpur (once in Allama Mashriqi's Khaksar Tehrik). (*Dawn*, Karachi, Pakistan, March 27, 1971.)

[94] *Dawn*, Karachi, Pakistan, March 27, 1971.

[95] Col. Akhtar Ahmed Khan (brother of Dr. Akhter Hameed Khan) received commission in the Indian Army almost the same time as General Tikka Khan, 1941 and 1940 respectively. Both were good friends and met in 1971. General Tikka claimed to Col. Khan that he had succeeded in crushing the insurgency in East Pakistan. Nevertheless, ground realities, including his replacement by General Niazi, do not speak loudly of General Tikka's claim.

[96] *The Report of the Hamoodur Rehman Commission Of Inquiry into the 1971 War [as Declassified by the Government of Pakistan]*. Lahore, Pakistan: Vanguard Books Pvt. Ltd., p. 193.

[97] Ibid.

[98] *The Pakistan Times*, Lahore, Pakistan, March 28, 1971.

[99] Khan, Air Marshal (Retd.) Inam-ul-Haq. *Defence Journal*, May 2009.

[100] Masud, p. 541.

[101] Khan, Air Marshal (Retd.) Inam-ul-Haq. *Defence Journal*, May 2009, pp. 41-49.

[102] Khan, Air Chief Marshal Jamal A. *Dawn*, October 13, 2003.

[103] Masud, pp. 540-41.

[104] Khan, Air Chief Marshal Jamal A. *Dawn*, October 13, 2003.

[105] *1971 War In Pictures*. New Delhi, India: Publications Division Ministry of Information and Broadcasting,

Government of India Patiala House, 1971, p. last page. A few pictures of the surrender including of Mukti Bahinis are in this source.

[106] Shamim, p. 41.

[107] Khan, Air Chief Marshal Jamal A. *Dawn*, October 13, 2003.

[108] Sadiq, Usman. *PakDef Military Consortium*.

[109] Hali, Group Captain (Retd.) S.M. "A New Dawn." *Defence Journal*. http://www.defencejournal.com/2009-4/lte.asp. Last accessed November, 2014.

[110] "History of PAF: Pioneering Officers." *Pakistan Air Force* website. http://www.paf.gov.pk/pioneering_officers.html. Last accessed November, 2014.

"Air Commodore Mohammad Zafar Masud." *Indian Bharat Rakshak* website. http://www.bharat-rakshak.com/IAF/Database/Record/view.php?srnum=3314. Last accessed November, 2014.

[111] Hussain and Qureshi, pp. 44, 297.

[112] Masud, pp. 64, 550.

[113] Masud, p. 76.

[114] Hussain and Qureshi, p. 43.

[115] Hussain and Qureshi, p. 44.

[116] Masud, p. 557.

[117] Hussain and Qureshi, p. 301.

[118] Masud, pp. 528, 558.

[119] Masud, p. 558.

[120] Jinnah, Quaid-i-Azam Mohammad Ali. *Speeches as Governor-General of Pakistan 1947-1948*. Lahore, Pakistan: Sang-e-Meel Publications, 2004, p. 103.

[121] "'Mr. Jinnah is Acting as Omnipotent Authority'." *The Tribune*, September 11, 1941.

[122] I am an eyewitness that many people (including in the Defense Forces) in the West Wing used to look down upon Bengalis. In 1969, I went to East Pakistan and stayed with Dr. Akhtar Hameed Khan (Founder of the Bangladesh Academy for Rural Development and Orangi Pilot Project, Karachi, Pakistan) in Comilla. This was my first visit to Bangladesh. During my stay, I traveled to different cities and I noticed a sense of dissatisfaction, deprivation, and general resentment toward West Pakistanis among the Bengali population. If people came to know that I was related to Dr. A.H. Khan, I was treated with love and affection and they welcomed me with cheek to cheek smiles. However, respect for West Pakistanis was otherwise generally non-existent. Sadly, the powerful Pakistani establishment not only took Mashriqi's warning lightly, but kept ignoring the situation on the ground in the East Wing and continued making blunders over time.

[123] Hussain, Syed Shabbir. *Al-Mashriqi: The Disowned Genius*. Lahore, Pakistan: Jang Publishers, 1991, pp. 256-257.

[124] *Dawn*, Karachi, Pakistan, March 2, 1971.

[125] *The Daily Star*, Vol. 8, Issue 80, July 31, 2009. http://archive.thedailystar.net/magazine/2009/07/05/cover.htm. Last accessed December, 2014.

[126] *The Report of the Hamoodur Rehman Commission*, p. 85.

[127] *The Report of the Hamoodur Rehman Commission*, p. 89.

[128] *The Report of the Hamoodur Rehman Commission*, p. 507.

[129] *The Report of the Hamoodur Rehman Commission*, p. 183.

[130] BBC reported: "A court in Bangladesh has sentenced a well-known Muslim cleric [Abul Kalam Azad] to death for crimes against humanity during the country's 1971 independence war.

…The cleric, a presenter of Islamic programmes on television, shot dead six Hindus and raped Hindu women during the war, prosecutors said.

…Mr Azad was a junior leader in the student wing of the Jamaat-e-Islami party in 1971 and a member of the Razakar

Bahini, an auxiliary force set up to help the Pakistani army by rooting out local resistance.

The Razakars were notorious for their operations targeting Hindus as well as civilians suspected of being sympathetic towards Bengali nationalists." ("Bangladesh cleric Abul Kalam Azad sentenced to die for war crimes." *BBC News.* January 21, 2013. http://www.bbc.co.uk/news/world-asia-21118998. Last accessed December, 2014.)

[131] *The Report of the Hamoodur Rehman Commission*, pp. 193, 508.

[132] *The Report of the Hamoodur Rehman Commission*, p. 197.

[133] *The Report of the Hamoodur Rehman Commission*, pp. 285-312.

[134] After the embarrassing defeat, the morale of the Pakistani Defense forces was at its lowest point. After the war, an urgent and rigorous training program of PAF pilots and technicians began. For the first time, the importance of the fighter controllers was realized and as such, re-vamping of the Air Defense began. "Surface to air missiles entered the PAF arsenal for the first time..." (Masud, p. 60.).

[135] *The Report of the Hamoodur Rehman Commission*, p. 507.

[136] This report is 545 pages, published by Vanguard Books Pvt. Ltd, Lahore, Pakistan. It seems to be incomplete. At the time of presentation to late Prime Minister Zulfiqar Ali Bhutto, two volumes were presented and those appear to be at least as thick as the one published by the said publisher.

The published report has omissions and/or many important elements were not recorded. For example under: "Political history of Pakistan from August 1947 to 7th October 1958", nowhere does it mention how opposition leaders like Allama Mashriqi were crushed right after the creation of Pakistan. The report also omits Allama Mashriqi's warning regarding the separation of East Pakistan. It does not speak of the Muslim League's failure in the first elections. And it does not have any statements by Air Commodore M. Zafar Masud. By omitting such many important facts, the credibility of the report becomes questionable. This is also telling of the undemocratic methods right from 1947. The report has no index, which makes it cumbersome to locate the relevant information.

www.ingramcontent.com/pod-product-compliance
Lightning Source LLC
Chambersburg PA
CBHW020508100426
42813CB00030B/3160/J